THE GREAT AWAKENING

JOHN H. GAMBLE, JR.

AND

WILLIE J. THOMPSON, JR.

Printed in the United States of America

First Edition, 2023

HARDBACK ISBN: 978-1-0880-8572-1

PAPERBACK ISBN: 978-1-0880-8568-4

EBOOK ISBN: 978-1-0880-8571-4

Red Pen Edits and Consulting, LLC

www.redpeneditsllc.com

TABLE OF CONTENTS

NINE

TEN

INTRODUCTION

In my tradition the season of revival was during the hottest months of the year. Down in rural South Carolina, you could hear the sounds of common meter hymns, hands clapping, foot stomping and call and response preaching for miles around coming from African American faith communities with heisted windows. Preachers prepared and served their famous road sermons during June, July and August to waiting congregations with standing room only and in the warmest climates ever experienced where a handkerchief was a common accessory for both women and men who attended these spiritual camp-meetings.

As a northerner who grew up looking at the Statue of Liberty and the Twin Towers from the banks of the Hudson, five minutes from my impoverished neighborhood, the season of revival was never linked to a particular time of year. In many ways, revival was connected to the actual struggle of the people, and the availability of a preacher to come to our church and let those in attendance know that God had not forgotten about us. As a child, I wondered why there was a need for these extra services during the week when my mother and I went to church faithfully every Sunday morning. But what I did notice was that the energy and fervor of these services were different than the Sunday morning experience. Particularly, I noticed that those who seemed stone faced and disinterested on Sunday were more active and engaged. These scenes were different, but some were necessary.

I always associated heat with revival. As a young man when the temperature got hot I knew it was the signal that the revival circuit was about to begin. We went from Round Top Baptist, to Fort Clark Baptist, to Greenhill Baptist, to Shady Grove AME, to St. James AME, to Mount Moriah Baptist, and so on. I thought churches chose the summer time because it had some spiritual significance or connection to the cloven tongues mentioned in the biblical account of Acts, when the Holy Spirit descended and the birth of the Christ centered church took place. The heat must have been a sign of what was needed to restore the energy and ethos of bodies of called-out believers who somehow had grown cold in their pursuit of a Christ-centered life and a humankind-focused service. The heat descending in the Acts account for some reason, brought levels of understanding and identity for a diverse gathering of individuals who, after their upper room encounters departed and expanded that experience to homes and towns all over the world as it is today.

I associated revival with newness, a time to hear someone different. Growing up in Jerusalem Missionary Baptist Church, our pastor Rev. Dr. H. B. Percy was the consistent voice we heard every Sunday. He was protective of the pulpit and selective about who was invited to come and minister to our congregation. We did fellowship with other churches. We were also an active part of our district association, but we knew that there were few voices who would be allowed to come and preach to us. Actually, there are about five preachers I recall being consistently part of our church's fellowship. However, there was one that always stood out to me as my recollection of him accompanies a memory of my mother and other parishioners in praise – the revivalist.

But when I was called to write and decree revival, it was during the coldest time of the year in the region where I was called to serve. Temperatures were -8 and plunging. The trees and shrubbery were always overlaid with frost. Birds migrated to warmer climates and other animals have gone into hibernation. A few inches of snow would fall on a daily basis and the threat of hypothermia and frostbite was a reality for students and parents who had to face the morning cold. It was winter. Trees suspend growth. Seeds lie dormant and plant metabolism has the heart rate at just above code blue. It was winter and no one calls for revival in the winter. But I heard a most assuring voice say, "It's Revival! It's time to wake up. It's time to get up and get moving towards what you have been called to do." This proclamation expanded my understanding and increased my trust in The One who totally understands that Winter dormancy can also be about conserving nutrients. Literally in trees, recycling takes place at the moment the leaves prepare to fall to the ground.

I've grown to believe that there is no right or wrong time for revival, but as a creature of habit, I have typically scheduled revival in the first quarter of the year at our church, which means revival for us has typically coincided with the end of Winter and beginning of Spring. Revival seems to then represent transition and newness, a change in seasons, and perhaps a change in the season of our church's ministry. I will never forget when revival fell in the heart of January. I was excited as one of my church's favorite evangelists was slated to preach his second revival with us. Our church has progressed amazingly during my time serving as its Pastor. However, our church has a historical tendency that precedes my time as Pastor of what I call "ministry ebbs and flows." There are times when things are going very well; other times when doing the work of the church is like pulling teeth. We were experiencing the latter and it was a perfect time for revival. Then, it happened! Almost two feet of snow fell in New Jersey. A State of emergency was just lifted. Roads were treacherous. Conditions were unfavorable and no one was "having church." Our church, a converted bar, has no parking lot. On-street parking in Newark was a disaster. There was every reason to call off revival. However, we decided that revival was so needed, that we paid for bulldozers to come and remove the snow. We cleared enough snow to walk directly in the church and revival was still on. Needless to say, people trekked through the snow and braved the elements to come. It was powerful to see. There was a push within us, an urgency and desperation to come together. There was a yearning in our souls to be awakened. Perhaps something within us was dying. Yet, we were determined to come and be revived!

On these pages you will find biblical texts identified and presented by two brothers cultivated in diverse theological institutions and charged to bring a life-changing perspective and voice to those who dare to be awakened to their vocations and callings. These messages were shared on the platforms of major movements and from the pulpits of bold and justice seeking faith communities. These pages will charge you in the midst of any season and are like the "Bread of Heaven," that will feed you until you want no more.

W. Thompson Jr.

J. H. Gamble Jr.

-ONE-

Save Our Sons

1 Kings 17:17-24 (KJV)

17 And it came to pass after these things, that the son of the woman, the mistress of the house, fell sick; and his sickness was so sore, that there was no breath left in him. 18 And she said unto Elijah, What have I to do with thee, O thou man of God? art thou come unto me to call my sin to remembrance, and to slay my son?

19 And he said unto her, Give me thy son. And he took him out of her bosom, and carried him up into a loft, where he abode, and laid him upon his own bed. 20 And he cried unto the LORD, and said, O LORD my God, hast thou also brought evil upon the widow with whom I sojourn, by slaying her son? 21 And he stretched himself upon the child three times, and cried unto the LORD, and said, O LORD my God, I pray thee, let this child's soul come into him again. 22 And the LORD heard the voice of Elijah; and the soul of the child came into him again, and he revived. 23 And Elijah took the child, and brought him down out of the chamber into the house, and delivered him unto his mother: and Elijah said, See, thy son liveth. 24 And the woman said to Elijah, Now by this I know that thou art a man of God, and that the word of the LORD in thy mouth is truth.

I Trust God! Rev. John H. Gamble Jr.

1 Kings 17:17 – 24

Simple story. A father took his young son out and stood him on the railing of the back porch. He then went down, stood on the lawn, and encouraged the little boy to jump into his arms. "I'll catch you," the father said confidently. After a lot of coaxing and encouraging, the little boy finally made the leap. He jumped off the railing and when he did, the father stepped back and let the child fall to the ground. Visibly shaken and obviously hurting, the father then picked his son up, dusted him off, and dried his tears.

Then he said sternly, "Let that be a lesson (to you). Don't ever trust anyone." (Bernie May, Learning to Trust)

And I think this father messed his son up with this example, because if there is anyone a child should be able to trust, they should be able to trust their mother or their father. And this father in fact has set his son up to be challenged in his faith because he has taught his son not to trust. And we cannot have faith without trust, and we cannot have trust without faith. Faith says I believe in you. I am loyal to you and I have an allegiance to you. Trust says I have complete confidence in you. Faith is about devotion. Trust is about dedication. Faith is spiritual. Trust is relational.

And the problem with some of us is that we are seeking the spiritual connection with God, and forgetting about the relational connection with God. That's why there are some people who are running, shouting, speaking in tongues, and they have the form of spirituality, but their lives are not improving and progressing, because they are seeking a spiritual connection, without the relational. They want the experience, but not the intimacy. That's why I warn you to not let Sunday be the only opportunity you have with God during the week. Don't let coming to church be the only time you talk with the Lord. Because being in worship can connect you spiritually, but if you want your relationship with God, then it requires getting to know God outside of the worship experience. You have to talk to Him when there's no one else around. You've got to have some quiet time with the Lord.

And that's where we fall in the text. In the text, Elijah has just finished his quiet time with the Lord. The Bible says that God told Elijah that for three and a half years, it would not rain. He then tells Elijah that in this dry season that he needs to go to the brook Cherith, because there is water there and God lets Elijah know that He has commanded the ravens to bring Elijah food at the brook. Don't miss the trust and the relationship building. Cherith was a ditch and the river that more than likely supplied its water was the Jordan, which was not drinkable. But God tells him to come spend this time at a ditch and to drink the water. Not only that, God says to him that the ravens would feed him. Now ravens are scavengers. They feast off dead animals and carcasses. They are "dirty birds". But don't miss the message. God is in fact telling Elijah that when you trust me, I can bring you to a ditch, with water that is considered undrinkable, and with birds that eat the inedible, and I can change the circumstances to where you are fed and nurtured daily, even while everything else around you in dying. Don't miss Cherith! This brook should have been dried up immediately when the rain stopped. But, since Cherith still contained water in the midst of a dry season, then the water had to be coming from a powerful source. The source had to be big enough, wide enough, and deep enough to provide water in the midst of a drought. In other words, the source of the water had to be greater than the drought.

But not only that, He used ravens to feed him. Ravens are tough birds. They have the mentality that regardless of how hard things are, they will continue to search until they find food. Ravens are not an animal that will starve to death because they are too determined to back down.

And that's why Elijah needs this time alone with God, because God is trying to show Elijah that the source of your strength is greater than the source of your struggle. Scripture would say it like this: Greater is he that is in me than he that is in the world. God is showing Elijah that if you are determined, you will live and not die. And that's how we have to learn to trust God. We have to learn to trust God to the point where we believe without a shadow of a doubt, that no matter what we encounter we will live, and not die. We will overcome. We will be victorious.

God brings him to Cherith, the water flows in the rainy season, dries up in the dry season. But God wanted Elijah to see, and God wants you and me to see that regardless of the season, if we trust Him, God will sustain us. Life is like Cherith. Life has its high tides and low tides, its peaks and valleys, its good days and bad days, but the challenge is to trust God in every moment, and every circumstance. And some of us, we need to learn to trust God in every season. Don't just celebrate God in the good times…. When things are going well for you…. When you are on the mountain, but I challenge you to trust God in the dry season… tough times… when your relationship falls apart… unemployment runs out… your body is racked with pain… when you get that phone call at night that your child is in trouble… Trust GOD in EVERY circumstance!

And that's the difference between Elijah and the widow.

8 Then the word of the Lord came to him, saying, 9 "Arise, go to Zarephath, which belongs to Sidon, and dwell there. See, I have commanded a widow there to provide for you." 10 So he arose and went to Zarephath. And when he came to the gate of the city, indeed a widow was there gathering sticks. And he called to her and said, "Please bring me a little water in a cup, that I may drink."

The Bible says that she goes to get him the water.

11 And as she was going to get it, he called to her and said, "Please bring me a morsel of bread in your hand." 12 So she said, "As the Lord your God lives, I do not have bread, only a handful of flour in a bin, and a little oil in a jar; and see, I am gathering a couple of sticks that I may go in and prepare it for myself and my son, that we may eat it, and die."

See, this is the difference between her and Elijah. Zarapheth was in Sidon, and Sidon was the center of worship for idol gods, specifically, the god Baal. Baal was the fertility god and the god of the thunderstorm. Don't miss it! Here this woman was living in the midst of a drought. Her god was the fertility (crops) and thunderstorm (rain), but in the text, there is no food or no rain. She feels as though God has failed her, therefore, she is going to make some bread, feed her son and herself, and then die. Elijah knows what God can do because he has seen the benefit of trusting God.

Cherith was not the first time God provided for his people. Has God not provided food before? Ask the children of Israel (complaining about no food in the wilderness.... Morning, bread appeared like dew on the roses... quail started to run through the camp).

Here again, God shows that He is to be trusted. After she listens to Elijah, takes her flour and oil and splits it up to make thee cakes instead of two, the Bible says that they ate for many days,

16 The bin of flour was not used up, nor did the jar of oil run dry, according to the word of the Lord which He spoke by Elijah.

But let me suggest that the lesson that this woman learned about trusting God did not come because she was able to eat many days. Notice in the text that there is no change in her language. There is no affirmation of the prophet Elijah. She referred to the Lord as "Your God" in verse and she has not made another statement since. Here it is. God has provided for her and yet she still has not acknowledged him. So God has to push the envelope further in her life to bring her to faith. The shift in her faith comes not when she is fed, but when her son dies. When we look back at the text.

17 Now it happened after these things that the son of the woman who owned the house became sick. And his sickness was so serious that there was no breath left in him.

Now here the original concern was that there was only a handful of flour and a jar of oil, and because of that they were going to die of starvation. The drought has not ended. There is an abundance of oil and flour. Yet her son became sick, and he died. Her original issue was that they would die because they had no food. They get food and her son still dies. Here is what I see in the text. Unfocused faith will lead to a misunderstood miracle. In other words, this woman was focused on getting food because her god was the god of fertility. She missed the miracle of Elijah's God multiplying what she had, because she was willing to divide it to help someone else. Her failure to recognize what God had done, led her to taking for granted that everything was alright simply because they had food. I would dare to even suggest that she might have still believed that it was her god that made this happen.

And see when you do not trust God, you will not fully recognize what the Lord has done. Be careful who gets the credit for the blessings in your life. Be careful who you recognize as the source of your good fortune. Be careful who you acknowledge as the reason for your being. Because God will not share his glory!

Come here Isaiah. Isaiah 42:8 The prophet declares, *"I am the Lord; that is my name! I will not yield my glory to another or my praise to idols. See, the former things have taken place, and new things I declare.*

God deserves glory for what HE has done! And no one deserves God's glory! That's why I don't need anyone to tell me to praise God… worship God… When I think of what God has done… is doing… (who He has been in my life), it becomes an automated response that I must give him GLORY!

Perhaps, her silent ingratitude suggests that she has to go through the unnecessary inconvenience of her son's death, so she can understand that it is faith in God that brought her through the dry season. And sometimes God has to allow you to go through an even greater storm for you to appreciate that it was God that brought you through the first storm!

Here is the next piece I see in the text. Misplaced trust will cause you to become dependent and not delivered. Notice the text.

> *17 Now it happened after these things that the son of the woman who owned the house became sick. And his sickness was so serious that there was no breath left in him.*

Now, here is my problem. The text is not clear about the age of the son. But it would be reasonable to believe that the son is at least of age where we can speak. But yet in this text, the woman is doing all the talking and her son is saying nothing. She is doing the cooking, her son is doing nothing. The woman is leading the conversation; the son is silent. Culturally, a widow should be cared for by her sons. So, either the son is too young to speak or the son does not have the faith to speak.

That's why you have to learn to trust God, because if you don't trust God, you will start to allow other people to speak for you when you should be able to speak for yourself. This son was privy to the same conversations and had experienced those same miracles as his mother. Yet she is the only one talking. It's not that deep. If God has done the same thing for you as He has done for me, I am not going to allow you to speak on my behalf when I can speak for myself. Here it is! Don't be silent about your salvation. The same bread that saved the mother was the same bread that saved the son. And if the mother was not going to acknowledge that God did it, the son could have acknowledged it himself. And that ought to help somebody in here today because the truth of the matter is that nobody can speak for you and say what you believe about God, because nobody can tell YOUR story! Nobody can tell what God has done for you better than YOU!

Deliver me from people who need to have a spiritual mouth piece, deliver me from people who want somebody else to give their testimony. I have my own testimony. I can be my own witness for what the Lord has done. Is there anybody here who can say that nobody can tell my story like I tell it? After what I have been through… After what I have had to deal with… the fact that I am alive today is a miracle. The fact that I am here is a testimony that there is a GOD somewhere. I should be dead… strung out… messed up! But I am here!

I am not going to keep silent and let somebody else's faith speak for me. I love my mother, but she doesn't know all I've been through!... father…. Family and my friends…. I have my own story! And I can't depend on you to tell my story because there is even deliverance in telling my story!

12

When I tell somebody what God can do, when I tell somebody what the Lord has done, it's a reminder that God is still in the blessing business….. turning things around…. Working out things in my favor! Is there anybody here who can testify that things are turning around in your favor?

But then we have to trust God because Mistrust is contagious. Notice the text.

> *18 So she said to Elijah, "What have I to do with you, O man of God? Have you come to me to bring my sin to remembrance, and to kill my son?" 19 And he said to her, "Give me your son." So he took him out of her arms and carried him to the upper room where he was staying, and laid him on his own bed. 20 Then he cried out to the Lord and said, "O Lord my God, have You also brought tragedy on the widow with whom I lodge, by killing her son?"*

Here it is. The woman trusted her god. The son trusted the mother. And now Elijah makes a statement where it seems like he doesn't know who to trust! He says,

> *"O Lord my God, have You also brought tragedy on the widow with whom I lodge, by killing her son?"*

He says, "O LORD MY GOD"! That should have been enough to affirm him and alleviate his issues. But when the people surrounding you are confused, it will start to confuse you, no matter how strong you are. When you are surrounded by insanity, it won't be long before you start to feel insane. Elijah is questioning God. Elijah is like, "God, I know what you told me. I have been obedient. I know you are the source and I know you are the reason we are making it in the drought? Why would you bring us this far and allow her son to die?"

God, you have been with us the whole time, why would you leave us now!

Have you ever been there? Have you ever been in a place in your life where it seems like God has been there every step of the way and the next thing you know it seems like God backs up! It seems like God disappears. It seems like God is no longer interested.

Here is the faith breaker for Elijah. Here is the place where, if Elijah doesn't trust God, his faith will fizzle. The mistrust of the woman and the son can infect Elijah and God's prophet may become paralyzed.

What do you when your faith is challenged and you need to trust God in a way that you never trusted him before?

It's in the text and I am done.

> 21 And he stretched himself out on the child three times, and cried out to the Lord and said, "O Lord my God, I pray, let this child's soul come back to him." 22 Then the Lord heard the voice of Elijah; and the soul of the child came back to him, and he revived.

He stretched himself and he spoke over the very thing that caused him to doubt! (We don't know what to shout about).

He stretched himself. He did something unlike he had ever done before… that had never been done in scripture. He stretched himself. He did something different! He took the child from his mother, put the child in an upper room, and stretched himself over the child THREE times. The word stretched means to measure out. He extended himself so that he completely covered the boy. And that's the lesson of trusting God. You have extended yourself beyond what you see. You have to extend yourself beyond what you are up against. You have to extend yourself beyond the roadblocks you see in front of you.

But the part I like is that he spoke to the very thing that created the disruption in his faith.

"O Lord my God, I pray, let this child's soul come back to him."

In other words, rather than wrestling with it, he brought it to the Lord so the Lord could deal with it. Had this boy not lived, it would have caused pain and doubt not only for the mother, but also for Elijah. So Elijah said,

"O Lord my God, I pray, let this child's soul come back to him."

And when you trust God, you take the things that create doubt and disruption and you bring it to the Lord in prayer!

And what I like about God is that He hears our prayers and He answers our prayers.

The Bible says,

> *Then the Lord heard the voice of Elijah; and the soul of the child came back to him, and he revived. 23 And Elijah took the child and brought him down from the upper room into the house, and gave him to his mother. And Elijah said, "See, your son lives!" 24 Then the woman said to Elijah, "Now by this I know that you are a man of God, and that the word of the Lord in your mouth is the truth."*

Trusting God doesn't mean you will never doubt. Trusting God is having confidence in Him to even deal with your doubt. Doubt is human. Doubt is natural. I mean even Jesus had doubt.

In the Garden of Gethsemane he doubted. He stated, "Father, if it be your will, let this cup pass from me. Nonetheless, not my will, but your will be done." He doubted. He prayed, but he trusted the Father all the way to the Cross!

Call It Back To Life   Dr. Willie J. Thompson Jr.

1 Kings 17:17 – 24

Have you ever heard of the theology of retribution? It is the idea that good deeds are rewarded and bad deeds are punished. We found in Deuteronomy 28.

> *"If you listen obediently to the voice of God and obey all of his commands, God will bless you beyond measure and blessings will come down on you and spread out over you and overtake you."*

But if you don't obey the voice of your God and keep His commands, that which was intended to bless will become a curse. If you don't do what God wants, God will send a curse and confusion and contrariness down on you, and destroy you until nothing is left of you, all because of your evil pursuits that led you to abandon God and do it your own way.

Have you ever tried to give someone advice, and they did not listen because they know all the answers to everything and they are stubborn? Have you ever told someone something for their own good and they refused to listen and ended up in the mess that you tried to warn them to stay out of from the beginning? Have you ever had a conversation with a brick wall, and even though they listened, they were closed off, shut down, and rolled their eyes when you were finished. And believe it or not, once we learn something or a certain way it is hard to get our minds to open up to something different. But God has a way of opening up every mind, and has a way of tearing down stubborn walls and God has a way of getting through to us even when we refuse to open up to Him.

And the book of the Kings is a perfect backdrop and record of what happens when people try to do it their way instead of God's way. It is a perfect backdrop and record of the theology of retribution in action in the lives of Israel, and Judah and all the kings who have their rule over these divided kingdoms. It is a perfect backdrop and record that screams if you do what God wants you to do you will be blessed. But if you don't do what God wants you to do you will suffer, you will fail and you will be cut off.

The people in the text are on a journey, because they wanted a plan that God did not intend for them to have. There was nothing wrong with what they wanted; it is just that it is not what God wanted them to have. And sometimes in life, we can want things that we want and there is nothing wrong with wanting things that we want, but if it is not what God wants us to have, it may bring more sorrow than singing and more pain than pleasure. God's people in the books of Kings, wanted a king, and then when they got a King and out of 44 only 3 of them were half-way decent, and all the rest led them on a journey of highs a lows that proved to them Obedience to God's commands brings blessings, while disobedience to God's commands brings failure.

And at some point God wanted His people out of the roller coaster of ups and down and off the merry go round of good and bad days and off the bumper cars of bad decisions. Because what they asked for only drew them further and further away from God. And when we get too far

> God wanted His people out of the roller coaster of ups and down and off the merry go round of good and bad days and off the bumper cars of bad decisions.

from God, God has the responsibility to disregard theology (our way of understanding Him) and walk into sovereignty. Which means that God can do whatever God wants to do, whenever He wants to do it and make a way for His people. And I would rather be ruled by sovereignty over theology any day. And our focal passage is a perfect record of the power of God in action even when our theology says He should be halted.

In 1st Kings 17 a prophet on the run shows up in the village of Zarephath (a town known for idol worship, and under the curse of a drought). Upon arriving in the village there was a widow there who was gathering sticks. Elijah calls out to the woman, to give him a drink of water. While on the way to fetch the water, he also asks her for a piece of bread. The woman makes the prophet of God aware that she has only a handful of flour and a little oil in the jug and she is gathering sticks, so that she may return home to her son to cook their last meal and die (she knew retribution). Elijah says, don't be afraid, but go home, do as you said and make me a cake first and if you do this God will allow your supply to keep going until the rain returns (Elijah knew sovereignty). She went and did as Elijah said and God did what Elijah said He would do and the flour did not run out and the oil kept flowing.

The woman is experiencing theology again: if you do what God says to do, you can succeed, and if you don't do what God says to do, you can fail. But what happens when you are doing what God wants and something bad still happens. For the text lets us know that some time later the bible says, her son became very ill, and it was so bad that her son stopped breathing and died. And this is a problem! Because she is a widow, who was minding her business, and on her own path to dying,

> *If you do what God wants, things will be well with you.*

and then some prophet comes and changes her life and shows her that obeying God and the Man of God will turn things around for you. He showed her that if you do what God wants, things will be well with you. But what do you do when you are doing all you can, taking care of this strange man, making biscuits day and night from a supply of oil and flour, that will not run out. What do you do when you bear a burden for God and bad stuff still seems to happen? The woman was following the Word and the man of God and all of a sudden the only thing she had left, was now dead.

This does not line up with theology; this does not say all will be well if you follow God. Why are you doing this God? This is not the way it is supposed to be. Why are you allowing me to lose something so dear, and I'm doing all I can to please you? And this text provides a context to help us understand why God sometimes allows challenging things to happen to good people.

The Bible says that "*some time later the son became ill and died.*" I believe God wants us to understand that God allows things to happen to show us that the presence of the prophet and the presence of God's provision does not exempt servants from encountering loss.

The prophet lived with her and the provisions of God sustained her, but it did not stop suffering and loss. You can be in the center of God's will and things will happen that will challenge you. You can be serving the Lord with all of your might, and something will happen. And you are not alone. Job was righteous and something happened. Jesus was doing the will of His father, and something happened. Four little girls were in Sunday School at the 16th Street Baptist Church in 1963 in Birmingham, Alabama and something happened. Martin King had a dream and something happened. God's presence and God's provision does not exempt servants of God from encountering loss.

You can be a good singer and something will happen. You can be the highest giver and something can happen. You can be a humble preacher, a wise leader and a gentle doorkeeper and something can happen. You can have access to the prophet of God himself or herself, but that will not exempt you from

> *Something Can Happen!*

encountering loss or sustaining a blow that will shake your very foundation. She was a servant and death still came.

But not only does God allow this to happen to teach servants that the presence of the prophet and provision don't exempt us from encountering loss; it may also allow God; to show us that personal past sins and public profanation can't provoke prophetic pain.

The woman cried out,

> *"What have I done to you oh man of God, have you come here to remind me of my sin and kill my son," (17:18).*

She had some mistakes of her own (personal) and she live among a group of people (a Phoenician city, Zarephath) who had some sins of their own also… You see, she obviously had already condemned herself for what she had done, because when we found her in the text, she had already pronounced death on her life and the life of her son. When we found her, she was already convinced that the end was near. When we found her she was already preparing for the worst and thought there was no way out. Her husband had already died and now she and her son would join him. She was convinced that the drought was the theology of retribution in effect. She knew where she was, and that was the judgment for where she had been. And now her son has died and she is trying to figure out why, it must be her past; it must be her past mistakes.

But past mistakes can't provoke prophetic pain.

> # *Past mistakes can't provoke prophetic pain.*

What is prophetic pain? Some things you are going to have to go through because it is meet for the master's use (2 Timothy 2:21). Some things you will have to go through because it is from God and it will bring God Glory in the end. The Bible records these things must happen so that the will and word of God might be made manifest in the earth. If it's prophetic pain, it is for the glory of God and it will work out for good in the end.

But location is also a concern, because the land is cursed with a drought. It again allows God to teach us that public profanation cannot provoke prophetic pain. She lived in a city where the people worshiped the Canaanite god who controlled the storm and rain. She lived in the hometown of Jezebel who worshiped Baal, and Elijah the prophet spoke a word and caused the heavens to shut up as a slap in the face to the Canaanite god. His word was judgment and it had a force behind it so strong that he had to hideout in the enemy's camp. And now this woman has allowed this prophet to hideout in her house, and provide for her and her son when they were almost going to die. Now her son has died and it looks like it is the result of sin, that the people of the city are in, that made the prophet stop by. And when the prophet came to her house her son died. She could have assumed, this must be judgment for what we as a people have done.

And I will say again, that public profanation cannot provoke prophetic pain. This woman losing her son was the prophetic plan of God all along, to bring her and us to this moment where God has to demonstrate not only His presence in the prophet, not only His provision of a meal, but also His power as the resurrection and the life. And neither the public nor the past can stop God from working it out for you. The pain is for His power to show up. The pain is for God to prove to His people that He is sovereign.

This pain is prophetic; God is going to use it to do something in the life of somebody. It's prophetic; it has the power to spark change in your children and family. You would have never come out of that if you did not get hurt. You would have never stopped that if the pain would have never come. You would have never stopped running, and jumping and dipping and diving, until you hit that brick wall that made you sit down and start listening to somebody that could show you a better way. That was prophetic pain and it was necessary so that you can help somebody else not go through what you went through.

The widow of Zerephath, is trying to understand what in the world is going on and why she has lost her son, and the Bible says the prophet takes the boy, takes him to the upper room and lays the boy on the bed of the prophet. And the prophet cries out to the Lord, "*Lord why have you brought tragedy to this woman, I live with, by killing her son.*" And the Bible says, "*Then he stretched himself out on the boy three times and cried to the Lord, Oh Lord my God Bring this Boy Back To Life,*" And the Lord heard him, and the boy started breathing again.

Ok that's it! The boy is back to life, thank you Jesus. But why did God allow this to happen? I want to suggest that God allows this to happen to show us that a prophetic prayer can provoke the pick up and pull through of the powerless.

Elijah is God's prophet, and has the strength of heaven backing him, but in his hands lay a powerless baby, a vulnerable baby, a baby boy who is in need of rescuing. Elijah stretches out over the baby boy once and that didn't work. Elijah stretched out over the baby twice, and that did not work either. Elijah stretches out a third time, and that does not work either.

But I would like to suggest that God didn't call him to extend himself to the full length or extent. God did not call him to reach from one point to another. God did not call him to spread out, dilute or lie down. God called him to speak. He is a prophet of God, called to speak the word of God over situations. God didn't ask him to stretch, you know, stretch your budget. God didn't ask him to stretch, you know, overextend yourself, trying to save people that don't want to be saved. God didn't ask you to stretch, you know, stretch the truth to make yourself look better and the story more dramatic…

God didn't call him to stretch, God called him to speak. The Bible clearly states that when the Lord heard Elijah's voice, that's when God responded. He had to remember that God calls the prophet to root out, to pull down, to build and to plant. But you have to do it with your mouth (Jeremiah 1:10). The Lord put the word in the mouth of the prophet. He has to remember that the power of life and death is in the tongue (Proverbs 18:21).

Elijah cried out "Lord God, bring this boy back to Life!" And when he prayed this prophetic prayer, it provoked a pick up and pull through for the powerless. It's time to speak life into situations and stop speaking death. It's time to call some things back up instead of putting things down. It's time to speak well of your future and stop speaking doom. It's revival. When you open your mouth you provide the way for something that is weak to get strong. When you open your mouth you provide the way for something that is broken to become fixed. The power of life and death, Elijah, is in your tongue. Stop stretching and start speaking. I am what God says I am!

I'm not bound, but I'm free. I'm not lost, but I'm found. I'm not down, but I'm up. I'm not sick, but I'm well. I'm not poor, I'm rich. Stop stretching and start speaking. And don't just speak to your situation. Be like Elijah, and speak to someone else's dead situation. Pray the prophetic prayer and provide a pick up and pull through for those who have no power. Your prayer is the pick up and your prayer is the pull through.

And when you do it, the boy will come back to life. And when Elijah returns the boy back to his mother alive, the woman declares, *Now, I know for sure, that you are a man of God, and that the Lord truly speaks through you.*

The widow's son that was dead, is now alive. She had food, she had a home, she was alone but making it the best way she knew how, but what broke her was the loss of her son. And when she lost him there was a prophet of God that God needed to prove to her and us was real through demonstration power. Could it be that we are going from a generation who only needed God to provide to a generation of people who need God to demonstrate God's power by bringing things back to life?

Could this be a generation that needs to hear, "Come back to Life." And I came to pronounce this day, at this time: It's Revival.

Call It Back To Life.

-TWO-

2 Kings 4:35 (KJV)

35 Then he returned, and walked in the house to and fro; and went up, and stretched himself upon him: and the child sneezed seven times, and the child opened his eyes.

Necessary Pain   Rev. John H. Gamble Jr.

2 Kings 4:8 - 37

David, a 2-year old with leukemia, was taken by his mother, Deborah, to Massachusetts General Hospital in Boston, to see Dr. John Truman who specializes in treating children with cancer and various blood diseases. Dr. Truman's prognosis was devastating: "He has a 50-50 chance." The countless clinic visits, blood tests, intravenous drugs, the fear and pain--the mother's ordeal can be almost as bad as the child's because she must stand by, unable to bear the pain herself. David never cried in the waiting room, and although his friends in the clinic had to hurt him and stick needles in him, he hustled in ahead of his mother with a smile, sure of the welcome he always got. When he was three, David had to have a spinal tap--a painful procedure at any age. It was explained to him that, because he was sick, Dr. Truman had to do something to make him better. "If it hurts, remember it's because he loves you," Deborah said. The procedure was horrendous. It took three nurses to hold David still, while he yelled and sobbed and struggled. When it was almost over, the tiny boy, soaked in sweat and tears, looked up at the doctor and gasped, "Thank you, Dr. Truman, for my hurting."

This young man believed that he would get better, but understood that there could be no healing except for if there is pain. It seems cruel that in order to get better, sometimes you have to feel worse. In order for God to add to your life, sometimes He has to subtract from your life. Fantasia puts in perspective, when she says, "Sometimes you gotta lose to win again."

What am I saying? There is a unique relationship between pain and faith that cannot be ignored. Most of us have the faith we have because of the experiences we have been through. It's when we go through, and we get through that we believe what God can do.

CS Lewis says in his book The Problem of Pain, "We can ignore even pleasure. But pain insists upon being attended to. God whispers to us in our pleasures, speaks in our conscience, but shouts in our pains: it is his megaphone to rouse a deaf world." In other words, if you want to become stronger in the Lord, (shift in your life, your calling, your ministry), pain is necessary.

No one desires pain. No one wants to be hurt. But when you ignore your pain, you set yourself up for permanent damage. Former NBA basketball star Bob Gross wanted to play despite a badly injured ankle. The team doctor injected him with Marcaine, a strong painkiller, in three different places of his foot. Gross started the game, but after a few minutes, as he was battling for a rebound, a loud snap! could be heard throughout the arena. Gross, oblivious, ran up and down the court two times, then crumpled to the floor. Although he felt no pain, a bone had broken his ankle. By overriding pain's warning system with the anesthetic, the doctor caused permanent damage to Gross's foot and ended his basketball career.

Because pain is a warning system for the body. Dr. Paul Brand, in the article, "Why is Pain Necessary?" says, "Ninety-nine per cent of all the pains that people suffer are short-term pains: correctable situations that call for medication, rest, or a change in a person's lifestyle." In other words, when you feel pain, it is a warning that something must be done or needs to happen to make you better.

Sadhu Sundar Singh says it like this.

A newborn child has to cry, for only in this way will his lungs expand. A doctor once told me of a child who could not breathe when it was born. In order to make it breathe the doctor gave it a slight blow. The mother must have thought the doctor cruel. But he was really doing the kindest thing possible. As with newborn children the lungs are contracted, so are our spiritual lungs. But through suffering God strikes us in love. Then our lungs expand and we can breathe and pray.

Let me argue that that is where we are in the text. In the text, we encounter a woman of Shunem, whose seems to have it all together. She is well-off, hospitable, and recognizes Elisha as the prophet of God. She seems to be a woman who has it all together, but yet in her story, she is blessed with a son, whom then dies, and is brought back to life by Elisha. Here she is this good woman. She seems to do everything right in the text. She seems to be the picture of what a believer should look like, and how a believer should act. And when I've heard this text preached, she is often lifted up, and celebrated for all that she did for Elisha. And it's been made to suggest that with all that she did for Elisha it was cruel for God to bless her with a son, only for that son to die. But let me suggest that there are some lessons about faith that could have only come through her pain. And if we just carefully review the text, I am sure there are some lessons for us in the text.

For example, she needed to understand that she needed Elisha more than Elisha needed her. Look at the text.

8 Now it happened one day that Elisha went to Shunem, where there was a notable woman, and she persuaded him to eat some food. So it was, as often as he passed by, he would turn in there to eat some food. 9 And she said to her husband, "Look now, I know that this is a holy man of God, who passes by us regularly. 10 Please, let us make a small upper room on the wall; and let us put a bed for him there, and a table and a chair and a lamp stand; so it will be, whenever he comes to us, he can turn in there."

Now, don't miss the message. I am not discrediting her hospitality. She did not have to offer him food or a place to stay. But this was a wealthy woman. She had plenty of means. She was not giving sacrificially; she was giving of her surplus. She was not like the woman in 1 Kings 17, who only had some flour and a jar of oil. She wasn't like the widow of Luke 21 who only had a couple of coins. This woman had it all together. She was rich and substance. And sometimes the danger of having a lot is that we become comfortable, and not thankful. So, God has to take from us something that we really value so we can understand that we need Him, more than He needs us. I know that's tough to swallow. I know that we don't like to hear that. But that's what God does! Even when you have faith, even when you are doing the right thing, like this woman, God can still subtract from your life something or someone of value so you can learn to lean on Him and not on what He has given you.

Isn't that the story of Job's life in a nutshell? He was a righteous man. He loved God. He stayed away from evil. Yet, God allowed Job to lose his health, his wealth, and his children so that he could understand that true faith understands that we need God more than God needs us! And I don't know about anyone else, but I can testify that I need the Lord! (I am not by myself! All of us in here should be able to say, "We need the LORD!")

She needs Elisha more than Elisha needs her. But then she had to realize that we should never second guess God. This woman was kind to Elisha and his servant Gehazi. They wanted to repay her kindness and she said that she was content with what she had. That was a good answer. But then they noticed that she was a rich woman with no son. No son means no heir to all the possessions they had. So, they promised her what, in that time, was the greatest gift a woman could receive – a male son. (Think back to the story of Hannah and how she prayed for a son). The Bible says that Elisha called the woman and,

16 Then he said, "About this time next year you shall embrace a son."

Look at her response.

And she said, "No, my lord. Man of God, do not lie to your maidservant!" 17 But the woman conceived, and bore a son when the appointed time had come, of which Elisha had told her.

The prophet of the Old Testament was clearly understood as the messenger of God. God's words spoke from his mouth, when she questioned the integrity of his prophecy; she was in fact, questioning God. When she said Elisha was lying, she was in fact, calling God a liar. And she should have been familiar with the scripture. Numbers 23 tells us God is not a man that he should lie; neither the Son of man, that he should change his mind. If God says it, He will do it. If God speaks on it, He will make good on it.

And too many of us forget that the promises of God are yes, and amen. Too many of us forget that if we pray about it and God reveals it to be so, if we are faithful and do not doubt, it shall come to pass.

So, she has a child, and then loses the child to give her another opportunity to get it right. And she doesn't do much better the second time. When the child dies, she runs out to Elisha and accuses him of deceiving her. But then as Elisha makes his way back to the house, she makes a statement that shows that she has learned her lesson. She says, verse 30,

"As the Lord lives, and as your soul lives, I will not leave you."

Her statement shows her determination. It shows her understanding that if God blesses me the first time; the only way I will be blessed again is if I stay with the Lord. And the pain that we go through teaches us that we need to stay with the Lord. It is easy to quit. It's easy to give up. It's easy to say I am going to stop having faith. But I have learned that even though it may hurt, my change comes when I stay with the Lord. Jacob had that testimony when he wrestled with the Lord all night. Hip broken. Bone displaced. But he was determined. Told the angel, "I will not let you go until you bless me." And he was changed! And that's why pain is necessary because it will push you to hold onto God. It will push you to stay with the Lord!

It is through my pain that I have grown stronger in the Lord. It is through my hurt that I've strengthened my relationship with Him! It's through losing loved ones that I've grown closer to Him… losing family and friends… dealing with hurt feelings… lies… rumors… stress… pressure. That's what has drawn me closer to the LORD!

Her son dies; she learns that she needed Elisha more than Elisha needed her. She learns that she can't second guess God, but watch this. She learns that she is connected to the close-minded. One of the issues in this text is not just the woman; it's her husband. The text says that they have no children. And I like the implications surrounding her barrenness. It says in the text,

And Gehazi answered, *"Actually, she has no son, and her husband is old."*

Now she is not the first barren woman in the Bible. Sarah, Rebekah, Leah, Rachel, Hannah all at times had trouble conceiving. Meanwhile, their husbands had other children with other women. The only thing we get from the text about this Shunammite woman is that her husband was old. The word for OLD in the original language of the text means he had become old. In other words, older men have children. Abraham had his first child when he was 86, and Isaac when he was 100. In other words, the barrenness of this union was not about age, but about productivity. Her husband had become old. In other words, he was unproductive. Hence, the problem was she could produce, but she was connected to someone who was not a producer.

Well, let me take it a step further, because they ultimately have a son, but notice the text: the son gets sick with sunstroke while he is with the father. The son gets sick out in the field with his father and look at the father's response: "Take him to his mother." He stays in the field and sends the son back with someone else! This is who she is connected to!

Let me take it a step further. The son dies. The mother called to her husband, and said, (22) "*Send me one of the young men and one of the donkeys, that I may run to the man of God and come back.*"

Look at his response.

> *23 So he said, "Why are you going to him today? It is neither the New Moon nor the Sabbath."*

Do you see the problem? Your son just died! And you are worrying about waiting for a certain day or season to get help! The Sabbath was every 7 days. The New Moon was the first day of the month! Your son is dead and you want to wait until well after the point of death to get to God! Do you see who she is connected to!

And the reason why we experience pain in our lives has nothing to do with who we are; but it has everything to do with who we are connected to. Some of us are connected to cancerous people…. Infectious

32

situations... diseased individuals... unproductive people... And we experience pain, because they don't know how to handle their affairs. They don't know how to do what they need to do!

And some of us need to take the hint from our social media accounts! There are some people who need to be on your restricted list.... Block.... Unfriend and unfollow... who you need to take out of your circle because they are unproductive. They are not looking out for you and what God has blessed you with... and they don't understand that when you need the Lord, nothing is more important than getting to God!

Sometimes God has to allow pain in your life so you can learn to separate yourself!

So, pain is necessary because it helps us to see that we need God. We can't second-guess God. And we must separate from those who want to keep us away from GOD.

But the death of this young man is helpful for us because it shows us that pain is at times necessary for change to take place. Like little David in the opening illustration, his only chance to get better was to take the pain that came with the spinal tap procedure.

And the pain of this experience of this young man who moves from death to life gives us insight into how change takes place in us. The Bible says that when the woman told Elisha of her son's death, he told his servant to go to the house.

> *29 Then he said to Gehazi, "Get yourself ready, and take my staff in your hand, and be on your way. If you meet anyone, do not greet him; and if anyone greets you, do not answer him; but lay my staff on the face of the child."*

But look at what happened.

31 Now Gehazi went on ahead of them, and laid the staff on the face of the child; but there was neither voice nor hearing. Therefore he went back to meet him, and told him, saying, "The child has not awakened."

He had Elisha's staff. The staff in the biblical signs was a symbol of authority. In Exodus 7, Moses stands in Pharaoh's court. Aaron throws down his staff and it becomes a serpent. The magicians of Egypt bring out their rods and do the same thing. The Bible says that Aaron's rod swallowed up the other rods. David said thy rod and thy staff they comfort me, because he had the authority!

But Gehazi passes the staff over the boy's body and nothing happens. He had Elisha's authority, but he did not have Elisha's anointing. In other words, he had Elisha's permission to do it, but he did not have the gift God had given Elisha to do it. What are you saying? God does not honor us trying to do things that he has not anointed us to do. Even if you are given permission to do it, if it is not what God would have for you to do, it will not change! You can have the authority. But if you are missing the anointing, then you will have no power. That's why David was able to slay Goliath, not because he was given Saul's authority to fight. Because Saul's authority was in his armor that couldn't even fit David. David dropped Goliath because God had anointed him for the battle.

What are you saying, preacher? Don't allow people to push you up to do something that God has not ordained. You cannot change somebody's life or make things better for people if you are not operating according to God's will. You can prolong the suffering and pain in somebody's life by trying to help them when you have no knowledge of how to change their situation. In other words, Gehazi's responsibility was by Elisha's servant, not the boy's reviver! Just because you are gifted in one area doesn't mean that you can do everything!

Let me make it plain. A podiatrist is a specialist in medicine pertaining to the feet. If I have a problem with my instep, my arch, or my heel, then he can help. But if my heart isn't right, I don't need a podiatrist; I need a cardiologist. The podiatrist can't use what he knows about my feet to help me with my heart. I need somebody who understands septum, valves, blood vessels, aorta, chambers. I need somebody who gets murmurs and atrial fibrillation. I need someone who gets cardiac care and coronary disease. Somebody needs to get this! Just because you have the authority to do something, doesn't mean that God has anointed you to do it. You can kill somebody's spirit. You can snatch somebody's joy by operating in areas that God has anointed you to lead or serve in. Just because you have permission doesn't mean God has given you purpose!

Sometimes we need to pray more about where God is leading us, so we don't end up killing more people than we are saving!

If God has not anointed you with a spirit of kindness, then you can't be an usher, nurse, or hospitality worker.

If God has not anointed you with a spirit of giving and service, you can't be a missionary or pastor's aide member.

If God has not anointed you with a spirit of leadership as well as humility, you can't be a leader in the church.

Just because you have the authority doesn't mean you have the anointing!

If change is going to take place, we have to understand that we need both authority and anointing, but then we also need to understand that if change is going to take place, we have to be completely covered.

32 When Elisha came into the house, there was the child, lying dead on his bed. 33 He went in therefore, shut the door behind the two of them, and prayed to the Lord. 34 And he went up and lay on the child, and put his mouth on his mouth, his eyes on his eyes, and his hands on his hands; and he stretched himself out on the child, and the flesh of the child became warm.

It is believed that the child may not have been an adult, but he was in his teen years. He was of full size. Therefore, Elisha, like his predecessor Elijah, had to lay over the boy to bring life back into the boy. The Interpreter's Bible says, "Only the uttermost giving of self can breathe the breath of life into the otherwise dead... It was by Christ's stretching of himself upon the cross of his infinite sacrifice that he brought to life again men that were dead in their trespasses and sins." In other words, this text is showing us God's willingness to cover and revive the dead parts of our lives. But the problem is not God, it's us. Unlike the boy who was dead and did not move, thus allowing Elisha to cover him completely, some of us have post mortem spasms. Some of the pain we deal with in life is because there are areas of our lives we don't want God to cover. We move some areas of our lives away from God, rather than asking him to bless all of it. We want God to cover our finances, but we don't want him to deal with our habits. We want God to cover our family, but we don't want him to cover our relationships. In other words, we don't want God in everything, only some things because we understand that part of resurrection and restoration is purification.

It is suggested that the boy died of heatstroke. Often with heatstroke comes infection. Therefore, if he died of sunstroke (heat stroke), in order for him to live, not only must the sun stroke be rectified, but also the infection that comes with it. What am I saying? When you don't ask God to cover all areas of your life, you might be leaving out the area that needs the most focus…. Is causing the most pain…. Is the real issue. See if you know anything about pain, the place of pain is not always the source of the pain. Just because you have a headache, doesn't mean that the problem is in your skull. There are numerous afflictions that can occur to your body that will cause pain in your head. So, if you only give God what hurts, then you may in fact be holding on to the real source of your pain. That's why if you want to be revived, and restored, you have to give God everything! You have to put it all in HIS hands!

If you want change to come, after dealing with necessary pain, then you can't settle for partial progress. Look at the text.

> *And he stretched himself out on the child, and the flesh of the child became warm. 35 He returned and walked back and forth in the house, and again went up and stretched himself out on him; then the child sneezed seven times, and the child opened his eyes.*

He could have been satisfied when the body became warm. But the text says that he went back a second time and stretched out on him again. The first time was enough to get him warm, but it was the second time that caused him to open his eyes. And look at what happened between him getting warm and opening his eyes. The Bible says he sneezed 7 times! We sneeze to get rid of foreign particles in our nostrils so we can breathe clearly.

God is committed to us living. And so as Elisha worked on the boy, Jesus works on you and me. And so, if we become content to just be warm, then we run the risk of dying again because we can't breathe. The Bible says that he stretched out on him again. And that's really where I want to end this message. Thank God that he is willing to keep working on me. Thank God that he has not given up on me. Thank God that he still sees some greatness in me where He is not settling for partial progress. And if I allow God to completely cover me and work on me, I can be like the boy who was presented to his mother when the prophet said,

"Pick up your son."

Be encouraged in knowing that the pain you've endured is only indicative of the change that God is sending you through! After all, the pain of this woman and the pain of her son does not compare to the pain that Jesus endured for us on the Cross. His pain was necessary for the salvation of the world! The prophet Isaiah said it best:

He was wounded for our transgressions, bruised for our iniquities; the punishment that made us whole was upon him, and with his bruises we are healed!

It's Revival   Dr. Willie J. Thompson Jr.

2 Kings 4:8 - 37

Every now and then in life, when something good happens to you at the hand of someone else; it may be in your best interest to return the favor. Major corporations all make major money and a portion of that money should be reinvested or given back to the community just as a favor. The Target Corporation in 2017 invested 9.7 million to the Twin Cities, just to establish art and social service initiatives by non-profit orgs. Google AdWords, gives 10,000 a month to non-profit organizations who want to advertise the mission and initiatives on Google as a way of giving back to the community in which they serve and profit from. Did you know that in 2012 alone Xerox contributed $13.5 million to Education/Workforce Preparedness, Science/Technology, Employee/Community Affairs, Cultural Affairs, National Affairs and Environmental Affairs, just as a way of giving back to the community. SHELL the Fuel and Energy corporation, gives away over 5 Billion a year in community, educational and environmental grants to organizations who help change the world in those areas, just as a way of giving back to their community. They do it to return the favor for so many people using their fuel and energy to mobilize their lives. Oh and the young people love Hip Hop. Hip Hop Artist Ludacris gave 20k to his alma mater, Banneker   High School in DC, to help support classrooms. Mary J. Blige started a women's empowerment center in Yonkers and is a mentor to young ladies in the Bronx. Brad Pitt, and Angelina Jolie, gave 8 million to the reconstruction of New Orleans. Denzel Washington gave 1 million to Wiley College, an HBCU in Texas. Alonzo Mourning gave 7 million to nonprofits who serve at-risk-youth. And Oprah is the black billionaire, who sponsors projects all over the world and started a leadership academy for Girls from every nation. Every now and then in life, when something good happens to you at the hand of someone else, it may be in your best interest to return the favor.

The people who understand the concept of returning the favor possibly understand the law of sowing and reaping. I think at the onset of today's text we encounter the concept of

> *The people who understand the concept of returning the favor possibly understand the law of sowing and*

returning the favor. A very wealthy woman, who lives in the town of Shunem, takes time to invite the prophet of God, Elijah, to a meal. From then on every time Elijah would pass that way, he would stop there to eat. But for this woman stopping and having a meal was not enough. So she encouraged and convinced her husband, saying,

> *"I am sure this is a man of God, who comes to eat with us from time to time, let's add another room onto the house," so that the man of God can have a place to stay whenever he comes by."*

And this brother must have been of African descent and recognized, you don't ever come in between a woman and her church and her man of God. (Hint, Hint). If you want her, you better come to church. If you want her, you better not just listen to her about her church, you better be prepared to write the check to make it happen." Because you don't ever want to get in between or tarnish or distract a woman's relationship between her church and her man of God…

The woman in our text convinces her husband to not only build a room on the house, but also fully furnish it with a bed, a table, a lamp and a reclining chair.

He understood a happy wife equals a happy life.

And this woman was simply like the corporations (metaphorically) in the introduction, that have come to a place of excess and want to share or simply return the favor for her being blessed.

Don't you know, it's a blessing to get the man of God in the neighborhood? It helps the community. Don't you know it's a blessing to get the man of God at the table? It provides opportunities to fellowship with somebody that has a word from the Lord. When the man of God is there everybody is blessed. Let's take it a little further, the man of God is symbolic of the Christian and God's Church. Don't you know there is a Christian and God's Church in your neighborhood? It helps the community be blessed. Don't you know, it's a blessing to get the Christian and God's Church at your table? It will provide you an opportunity for fellowship with someone who represents God, knows God and may have a word for you from God. Do you know how blessed you can be if you just take the person beside you to lunch? And I'm not talking about the Goonies, Goody-two-shoes and Gossips. I'm talking about someone who knows The Lord in the free pardon of their sins, and may have a WORD from God. For YOU... Ask your neighbor, "Take me to lunch... Take me to lunch." And not because you need something but just because you want to return the favor.

The Bible says, *"one day Elisha returned to Shunem, and he went up to the room to rest. He said to his servant Gehazi, "Tell the woman, I want to speak to her." When she arrived, Elisha said to Gehazi, "tell her we appreciate the kind concern she has shown to us. Now ask her what we can do for her. Does she want me to put in a good word for her with the king or to the commander of the army?"*

Here in the text the woman has been good to the Man of God, and one day the Man of God returns to Shunem and wants to simply return the favor.

> The law of sowing and reaping will manifest.

And I want to encourage you, that one day, the law of sowing and reaping will manifest, will show up, jump off in your life, and what you put out is going to be returned to you. But you must remember the law; you may sow a seed, but you are going to reap a tree.

Elisha wants to do something, so much more for her than she has done for him. And when what you have sowed comes back, it will be so much more than what you initially gave or sacrificed in the beginning. I dare you to get a seed and plant it, because it is going to come back greater than it was given.

Here it is again, the woman simply wants to bless somebody and here it is the prophet simply wants to return the favor.

The woman replies, "*No, my Lord, I don't need anything, my family takes good care of me. And have no need of anything,*" I just want to return the favor of prosperity and security in my life. I just want to be a blessing. I don't want anything in return.

But the man of God is desperate to find something that he can do to bless the woman, and return the favor. I imagine that he walks the floor, going to and fro, thinking what can he do to bless her back for all that she has done. I can see God walking back and forth in the great beyond, stressing over the blessing he is trying to get to you and I. Elisha thinks and thinks and thinks. And Elisha eventually asks his servant Gehazi, what can we give to her, and Gehazi, says, *She has no child*. That's it. We will ask the Lord will bless her with a child. He calls the sister and the sister stands in the doorway.

(Notice: her posture; Because what she was doing was a pure blessing, she didn't just BUST in the man of God's room, because it was her house. She was not trying to prove that she was in charge even though she brought the blessing to pass).

She stands in the doorway and the man of God says, *by this time next year you will be holding a son in your arms*. And the woman says, *"No my Lord, Please don't lie to me like that*. But sure enough the woman became pregnant, even with an old husband, and the following year she had a son, just as Elisha had said.

It was true. It really happened. It really came to pass. She was a blessing and got a blessing. She was just trying to help somebody else, and then somebody else came along and helped her. She gave of her excess and all of a sudden, she was given access. She was not trying to get anything in return, but she got everything she could have ever wanted. She was not only a wealthy, secure, married woman, but now because of her gift, she has become a mother. She was happy. She did what was right and was rewarded appropriately.

The Bibles, *"One Day, when her child was older, he went out to visit his father, who was working with the harvesters. Suddenly, he complained, "My head hurts, My Head Hurts." So the father said to one of his servants, "Carry him home to his mother," So the servant took him home and his mother held him on her lap. But around noon time, He Died.*

What Do You Do When The Blessings Backfire?

What do you do when the promise dies? You didn't ask for it, but since you got it and had it, for some time, you have grown accustomed to having it around. But what happens when you have put your time into something, you thought you would have for a lifetime, and it fails? What happens when you put your hope in somebody and they disappoint you? What happens when you cross all the T's and dot all the I's and still you come up unfulfilled and empty? What happens when you invest all you can in your children and they come back and disrespect you so bad, until you wish you were dead? What happens when you work hard and still fail? What do you do when what was given to you as a favor, becomes your worst nightmare, and dies on your lap? It was in your care and died. It was in your possession and died. It was under your leadership and died. You were supposed to take care of it and all of a sudden it died. It was fed by you and dressed by you and covered by you and here it is on your lap and its dead.

Have you ever had something you enjoyed and was grateful for and it died on you? If so, today's text comes to help you understand and potentially get a revival for a dead thing. It's Revival.

This woman provides a few things in the text we may need to see to help us gauge how we can revive the things in our life that have died while under our care.

That dream can come back to life. That child can come back to life. That parent can come back to life. That vision and that plan can come back to life. That marriage can come back to life. That anointing can come back to life. And the text may have a few things to share with us from this woman's perspective that may help us get a revival. In the text, notice a few things and let's celebrate.

The Bible says, *the boy died at noon time, the mother carried him up to the bed of the man of God, then shut the door and left him there.*" First I want you to notice, "She did not bury him immediately."

44

Some of us are in too much of a hurry to bury that which has been promised to us just because it has failed or died in our eyes. Now some things that are dead need to be buried. But if what has

> *Don't be in a rush to lose faith in something because it is not working the way you want it to work.*

failed in front of you was a promise, fulfilled for you, don't be in a rush to put it in the ground and move on. Don't be in a rush to lose faith in something because it is not working the way you want it to work. Sometimes you have to stay there until what died or failed is given a chance to be brought back to life.

She took her dead son and she did not run to the nearest cemetery. But the Bible says, she took him upstairs to the Man of Gods room that was built on to her house in the beginning of the story. Secondly, I want you to notice, She laid the boy (situation) in the place she prepared for God to rest.

She did not lay her son or situation anywhere. She laid him in a place where she had already prepared for God to show up and rest. She said "so that any time the Man of God comes into town, he can turn in here and rest." When what was given to us suffers or dies, we should already have a place prepared, where God can show up and God can sit down. It was dead, but she had already prepared a place for God to show up.

And someone asked me the other day, "Pastor, why are we fasting and praying?" I started to explain with a long answer. But today I can give the short answer. We are doing this to prepare a place for God to Show up and sit down. When you pray God shows up. When you fast God shows up. When you turn down your plate God shows up. When you do this as unto the Lord, God shows up. When you give, God shows up and when you get the nerve to build on a room in your house just for God. Guess what? God shows up.

Now since you have built the room, and have created some space in your life, and now that you have allowed your praise to build an altar for God, take that dead thing and Lay it THERE. You must have a place prepared for God to rest and show up, just in case your promise fails and dies on your lap.

The Bible says, she immediately sent a message to her husband: *"Send one of the servants and a donkey so that I can hurry to the man of God and come right back.* The Bible says, the husband asks "WHY TODAY!?" It's not the right time to inquire of the prophet of God. And the Message translation of the text gave us her sister girl's response, *"Don't ask questions, I need to go right now!"*

Thirdly I want you to notice, she did not give into the distraction. She was questioned about her doings, but she kept going for the Man of God. She did not have what she needed readily available, but she did not get distracted. She knew the situation, but she kept moving forward. And sometimes you have to learn to keep moving towards what you need, even when you are questioned. She did not give in to the distractions. Yes, it was not the right time, you are right sir; But I got to get to the Man of God. Yes, my child is home dead, but I cannot get distracted. Yes, my husband and my family don't understand why I do what I have to do, but I cannot get distracted. And she had the nerve enough to say, when she was questioned, It's alright and she kept on going. She did not get distracted, because she had a promise in crisis and when your promise is in crisis, DON'T stop for the foolishness, keep moving forward to where you need to be.

As she approached the man of God at Mount Carmel, Elisha saw her at a distance and said to Gehazi, *"Look, the woman from Shunem is coming. Run out to meet her and ask her, ``Is everything alright, with you, with your husband and with your child?"*

The woman told Gehazi, *"Yes everything is fine."* And there it is, My fourth thought is right here. She spoke well of a dead situation. *"Everything's Fine"* is what she said.

Sometimes as an act of faith, you have to speak well of your promise in crisis. Don't call your promise dead. Don't you let nobody call your promise dead. Don't you let nobody call your marriage, your family, your ministry, your anointing, your vision DEAD! When your promise has been put in jeopardy, say like she said, *Everything's fine*. We may be beat up, but *Everything's fine*. We may be struggling, but *Everything's fine*. We may be living paycheck to paycheck, but *Everything's fine*. You have to come to a peace in God, and a trust in God, where you can look at the dead thing and say *Everything is Fine*.

> *Don't You Let Nobody Call Your Promise Dead.*

Those were her comments to Gehazi (valley of vision), *"But when she got to the man of God, she fell to the ground before him and caught hold of his feet. Gehazi began to push her away, but the man of God, said Leave her alone." Something is troubling her deeply, and the Lord has not told me what it is." Then she said, "It was you my Lord, who said I would have a son. And didn't I tell you not to raise my hopes?"*

Notice in the text, my fifth thought is right there; She questioned the Master, but in a bowed position. And for some of us with promises in crisis, it is ok to question the Master. But we should go to Him like her, in a bowed position. She fell down on her face and asked the question. And sometimes when we get manifestations of God's word and promises, we feel we can treat God any kind of way, because we deserve what God did for us.

But she questioned the Master in a bowed position. She got down low, as a sign of respect and homage. I may not agree with what has happened, but I will not disrespect who you are. She got down low with her questions. Not puffed up but bowed down. Not prideful, but prostrate. Not with a sense of entitlement, but in a position of reverence. She had questions, but she humbled herself to the feet of the master and look at what happened.

Elisha tries to send Gehazi, ahead to solve the problem, but the woman said "No sir, I'm not going back without you." She said "I'm not going home unless you come."

And here is our next nugget: She refused to face the situation alone.

Sometimes we try to deal with this stuff on our own. But God has placed someone in your life that has the power and the word from God to help you with the crisis of your promise. But like this woman, you must refuse to face the situation alone. She told the prophet, You are going to have to come with me. I will not face this alone. And that's good news to somebody, who's been trying to hide by doing it all alone. You are exposed. When your promise is in crisis, refuse to do it alone. Find you one of the really good and saved and sanctified persons, and latch on and let somebody help you in the midst of your storm. You don't have to do it alone. You don't have to face it alone. You don't have to walk this road alone. Your promise is in trouble and you have to refuse to face it alone. Loneliness will lead you to depression and alcoholism. Loneliness can cause you to become suicidal. In children, loneliness is why they drop out of school, they become delinquent and antisocial. Lonely people have higher levels of stress and cannot rest even when they are resting. Lonely people have high blood pressure. And cannot sleep at night and spend less time in bed than the non-lonely. But you have to refuse to face the crisis of your promise by yourself. Like this woman, say I'm not going unless you go with me. She refused to face it alone.

Are you saved? Let me really see if you are saved? Or are you are playing Christian? Let me tell you what I'm really going through. And I'm not telling you just so you know, I'm telling you, because I'm not going back home, unless, you pray with me. I'm not going back home, unless you walk through this with me. I'm not going back home, unless you come with me, I refuse to face this alone.

"You're not leaving me behind" is what the woman said to the man of God, the church of God, people of God and the prophet goes back with the woman.

When the prophet arrives, he enters the room where the little boy is laying. He went in and shut the door. He prayed to the Lord. Then he laid down on the child's body, placing his mouth on the child's mouth, his eyes on the child's eyes and his hands on the child's hands. And the Bible says "The child's body began to grow warm again! Elisha got up and began to walk back and forth through the room a few times. Then he stretched himself out again on the child. And the Bible says, this time the boy sneezed seven times and opened his eyes! Then Elisha summoned Gehazi. "Call the child's mother, he said. And look what happens.....

And when she came in. Elisha said, "Here take your son!" She fell at his feet overwhelmed with gratitude. Then she picked up her son and carried him down stairs.

And here is the last thought of this message; She embraced what was brought back to life.

We have to be careful that when God moves and brings back what you thought was dead, you have to remember to embrace it. Sometimes people when they go off and fall and finally wake up and come back, we have a hard time embracing what was brought back to life. We sometimes enjoy people who get saved for the first time, but we sometimes forget to rejoice, when people who were once alive and somehow died, actually get a chance to come back by the power of God. Once what was dead came back to life, the woman embraced him and carried him downstairs.

And guess what. We were just like this boy. A promise to somebody. A blessing to somebody. A favor to somebody.

We were just like this boy, a miracle to somebody. But one day Something happened. We were out there in life and something happened. We once walked with God in the cool of the day, and one day something happened. Something came and took us out of our minds and took us out of our relationship with God. We were in God's care and still died. Under God's watch and still died. Living off of God's provision and Still died.

But God is like this woman who not only found a way for us to come back to life, but also became the way for us to come back to life. And God Himself, prepared himself a body, because we were dead in our sins and trespasses. God prepared himself a body, because we were a dream deferred and a promise in crisis. God decided to send his only begotten Son to die so that we could be brought back into relationship with Him. And He gave his life on a tree so that he could take our place in death and give us another chance at life. And when you confess the Lord Jesus and believe in your Heart that God has raised him from the dead, you are not only saved, but you are actually brought back to life. And when you come back to life. It is the job of God's Church, to embrace what was brought back to life. It is the job of the church to wrap their arms around you and return the favor. It is the job of God's Church to carry you to a safe place. It is the job of God's Church to say, welcome back. And like the mother in this text, and the Father in the Gospels, have a great big party, saying WELCOME HOME to my son who was dead and now alive …

> *We have to embrace what God has brought back to life.*

The woman responded in gratitude and picked up the child and carried him downstairs. We have to embrace what God has brought back to life. It's Revival. It's time to Wake up, and It's time to live. It's Revival. Come Back To Life…..

-THREE-

Kings 13:21 (KJV)

21 And it came to pass, as they were burying a man, that, behold, they spied a band of men; and they cast the man into the sepulchre of Elisha: and when the man was let down, and touched the bones of Elisha, he revived, and stood up on his feet.

It's Still In You   Rev. John H. Gamble Jr.

2 Kings 13:14 – 21

During the Vietnam War, David went through rigorous training to become part of the ultra-elite special forces team the Navy used on dangerous search-and-destroy missions. During a nighttime raid on an enemy stronghold, David experienced the greatest trial of his life. When he and his men were pinned down by enemy machine-gun fire, he pulled a phosphorus grenade from his belt and stood up to throw it. But as he pulled back his arm, a bullet hit the grenade, and it exploded next to his ear.

Lying on his side on the bank of a muddy river, he watched part of his face float by. His entire face and shoulder alternately smoldered and caught on fire as the phosphorus that had embedded itself in his body came into contact with the air. David knew that he was going to die, yet miraculously he didn't. He was pulled from the water by his fellow soldiers, flown directly to Saigon, and then taken to a waiting plane bound for Hawaii.

But David's problems were just beginning. When he first went into surgery—the first of what would become dozens of operations—the surgical team had a major problem during the operation. As they cut away tissue that had been burned or torn by the grenade, the phosphorus would hit the oxygen in the operating room and begin to ignite again! Several times the doctors and nurses ran out of the room, leaving him alone because they were afraid the oxygen used in surgery would explode!

Incredibly, David survived the operation and was taken to a ward that held the most severe burn and injury cases from the war. Lying on his bed, his head the size of a basketball, David knew he presented a grotesque picture. Although he had once been a handsome man, he knew he had nothing to offer his wife or anyone else because of his appearance. He felt more alone and more worthless than he had ever felt in his life. But David wasn't alone in his room. There was another man who had been wounded in Vietnam and was also a nightmarish sight. He had lost an arm and a leg, and his face was badly torn and scarred.

As David was recovering from surgery, this man's wife arrived from the States. When she walked into the room and took one look at her husband, she became nauseated. She took off her wedding ring, put it on the nightstand next to him, and said, "I'm so sorry, but there's no way I could live with you looking like that." And with that, she walked out the door. He could barely make any sounds through his torn throat and mouth, but the soldier wept and shook for hours. Two days later, he died.

That woman's attitude represents in many respects the way the world views a victim of accident or injury. If a trial emotionally or physically scars someone or causes him to lose his attractiveness, the world says "Ugly is bad," and consequently, any value that person feels he has to others is drained away. For this poor wounded soldier, knowing that his wife saw no value in him was more terrible than the wounds he suffered. It blew away his last hope that someone, somewhere, could find worth in him because he knew how the world would perceive him.

Three days later, David's wife arrived. After watching what had happened with the other soldier, he had no idea what kind of reaction she would have toward him, and he dreaded her coming. His wife, a strong Christian, took one look at him, came over, and kissed him on the only place on his face that wasn't bandaged. In a gentle voice she said, "Honey, I love you. I'll always love you. And I want you to know that whatever it takes, whatever the odds, we can make it together." She hugged him where she could to avoid disturbing his injuries and stayed with him for the next several days. Watching what had happened with the other man's wife and seeing his own wife's love for him gave David tremendous strength. More than that, her understanding and accepting him greatly reinforced his own relationship with the Lord. In the weeks and months that followed, David's wounds slowly but steadily healed.

It took dozens of operations and months of agonizing recovery, but today, miraculously, David can see and hear. On national television, we heard David make an incredible statement. "I am twice the person I was before I went to Vietnam. For one thing, God has used my suffering to help me feel other people's pain and to have an incredible burden to reach people for Him. The Lord has let me have a worldwide, positive effect on people's lives because of what I went through. I wouldn't trade anything I've gone through for the benefits my trials have had in my life, on my family's life and on countless teenagers and adults I've had the opportunity to influence over the years. David experienced a trial that no parents would wish on their children. Yet in spite of all the tragedy that surrounded him, God turned his troubled times into fruitful ones." (From The Gift of Honor)

Notice the difference between the two wives in the story. One could not see through the ugliness of what her husband had been through and walked away. The other saw through the ugliness to see her husband. Her husband was still there. She just had to see past what was in front of her.

And this is a good text to look at because this shows us a different Elisha than we have seen in the past. This is not the same Elisha who caused the head of an ax to float. This is not the same Elisha that caused oil to flow from the widow's jars until she could pay all of her debts. This is not the Elisha who instructed Naaman to dip himself in Jordan seven times. The Elisha we experience in this text is not like the Elisha we have seen before. (Last week we saw an Elisha that was healing a woman's son, but this week Elisha needs to heal himself.) Chapter 13, verse 14 says that Elisha had fallen sick of his sickness from which he would eventually die. Now what makes this text so powerful is that Elisha becomes sick at the time when he is needed the most. Israel has had two kings Jeho-ahaz and Jeho-ash, and both of them disobeyed God. And because of their disobedience, the nation was oppressed by the Syrians. Things were a mess. And if there was any point where the nation needed a word from the Lord, if it was any point where the nation needed a prophetic voice, it was now. But ELISHA is dealing with his own sickness!

And there is nothing more frustrating than when you are needed the most, to be at your weakest point. There is nothing more painful than to know that you are the agent for change, transformation, and healing, yet you are dealing with your own sickness, your own issues and your own demons, to where you don't believe that you still have it like you used to have it.

Let me suggest that Elisha gets to a point in the text where he allows his own sickness to compromise his confidence in what God had called him to do. How do I know this? Because Elisha's ministry was one where he experienced great success. Unlike Elijah before him where Elijah was running from Ahab and Jezebel, crying under juniper trees, on suicide watch, and drinking out of dried up brooks, Elisha was powerful and respected. He was able to walk into the king's court and have a conversation. When Elisha spoke, people listened. When Elisha showed up, it was evident that he did not walk alone, but that God was walking by his side. But now that he is sick, Elisha is not walking boldly, he is giving instructions from the bed. He is trying to encourage the king that he will be delivered from the Syrians, but the boldness from which he spoke in the past doesn't seem to be there in the present. And sometimes, when you are dealing with your own struggles, we tend to forget that the same God that called us is the same God that equips us, even in our worst state.

Elisha is not talking with the boldness that he has spoken with in the past. He is using metaphors with the king, telling him to shoot bows and arrows, which while figuratively connects with Joshua stretching his spear in victory (Josh 8:18), he doesn't move the same authority as he did before. And I just wonder when I read the text, "Has Elisha allowed his sickness to compromise his authority?" I wonder if Elisha, who was so used to success, and producing miracle after miracle, has he given up because he cannot do what he used to do? Or has he given up because he is sick and he is not the image of who he once was? Is he like the man in the opening illustration who died because his wife couldn't look at his scars? After all the text says that the king cried when he saw him. Did Elisha give up on his ministry and what God had blessed him with because of what he was going through. Because verse 14 proclaims him sick. He has one conversation and by verse 20 he dies.

And I just believe that some of us die in our spiritual lives because we allow our sickness to overtake us. Some of our dreams and aspirations die because we allow that which has infected us to destroy us. Here is a man, who was doubly blessed by God to serve God. He was a prophet to the nation, and one of the few prophets who could challenge the king and still sit at the king's table. Yet, when the nation needs him the most, and he gets sick, he dies. Here he is a prophet during the dark days of two kings Jeho-ahaz and Jeho-ash. The next king is going to be a man who does right in the sight of God. Perhaps, if he could have lived, he would have had opportunity to work with a king knew the Lord.

Here is what I am saying. Sometimes we allow a sickness, a situation, something we did not expect (let me put it like this – a life interruption) to make us think that our lives are over. We allow what happens to us, in Elisha's case, an unexpected illness, to become our death sentence, not realizing that we still have IN us all that GOD has given us.

It's Still In YOU!

Here's my argument for the text. Elisha dies before his time. He still has more God wanted him to do, but his illness kills him. Here's the sermon in a sentence: Don't let what AILS you kill What IN You!

Here's the text. Elisha is a prophet. The prophet always emerges in the biblical text to speak to the nation in crisis. Here is a nation with two wicked kings in a row. Now, there are being invaded. Elisha has plenty of work to do, but he is dead.

I mean, look at the text. We see three types of people who could have used a word from the Lord. First, there are people with a Moabite mentality. The Bible says,

> *20 And Elisha died, and they buried him. And the bands of the Moabites invaded the land at the coming in of the year.*

Remember how the Moabites came to be in the first place. The Moabites are a byproduct of Lot's experience in Sodom and Gomorrah. You remember the story. God sends Abraham out of Ur of the Chaldeans to the place he had prepared for him, but Abraham does not go alone. He brings his nephew Lot with him, who ends up being more of a burden than a benefit. His herdsman started arguing with Abraham's servants. He chose the more fertile land. He pitched his tent toward the worldliness of Sodom. And because Lot was focused on himself more than the Lord, Abraham has to save Lot from Sodom, and has to deal with unnecessary stress from someone whom he tried to bless. Can I just park right here and tell somebody that some of the stress that you are dealing with in your life is because you are trying to help somebody who may not want to be helped. Some of what you are dealing with might be the result of you trying to help somebody who already thinks they have the answers. The promise of God was for Abraham. God spoke to Abraham! If Lot was smart, he would have followed Abraham's leadership and reaped the benefits.

But Lot was so into himself, he ends up stuck in Sodom, where first Abraham saves him, then the Lord himself saves him, and destroys the city. His wife looks back and becomes a pillar of salt. Lot, out of fear, lives in a cave. His two daughters can't leave the cave to find a man, so they make their father their man. They get him drunk. They lie down with him. They get pregnant. And they give birth to two sons Moab and Ben-Ammi. Moab's children are known as the Moabites. Ben-Ammi's children are known as the Ammonites. And they keep fighting against the children of Israel, because like Lot was of Abraham, they remain envious of Israel. They fight with Israel. They are constantly trying to stop Israel's progress, but they fail to understand that you do not have to be jealous of what God has blessed others with. What you need to do is learn how to be connected to the people who can help you get to God would have for you to be.

You don't believe me. There is a precedent in the text. Ruth was a Moabite. We know her story. Israelite men married Moabite women, Ruth and Orpah. (TELL THE STORY) "Your people will be my people. Your God will be my God." She stays connected, and meets a man named Boaz.

Because we have to learn to put our jealousies, envies, and competition aside, and be connected and in community with people who can help us achieve what we desire for our lives. None of us are self-made. All of us needed somebody to help us get to where we are. Some of us have a job right now because of who someone we knew in human resources who hooked us up with the interview. Some of us were accepted into college, not because our grades were good, but because we knew someone who said, "Give her a chance."

The reality is that we all need somebody to get to where we are trying to go! We all could use help. And don't be made at the people who made to where you are. Connect yourself and try to learn something so you can get there!

We have to get over our Moabite mentality. We have to stop fighting the people, who have the very thing that we need. Just like Ruth, if the rest of Moabites would have connected to the Israelites the way Ruth connected to Naomi, they would have reaped the benefits that Abraham tried to give to Lot! We have to analyze who are the Boaz(es) of our lives. We have to find the Abrahams, God has given us and we have to stay connected.

There are some people whom I know God has connected with me. There are some senior pastors I know God has connected with me with. There are some leaders, some friends, some confidantes I know God has connected me with – not because they need me, but because I need them! Deliver me from this independent, "I don't need anybody" spirit! None of us can live in this world alone. None of us can do it by ourselves. It's okay to need somebody else!

There are people who will have a Moabite mentality. But then there are people who will want to have a Hand in Your Harvest. The Bible says,

> *20 And Elisha died, and they buried him. And the bands of the Moabites invaded the land at the coming in of the year.*

The key word is that word band. It means marauders, or raiders. In other words, this group of Moabites was thieves that only showed up at the coming of the year. In other words, harvest times. They were jealous people who didn't want to be helped, but then they wanted to help themselves to Israel's harvest! They did not want to work the land that they had in Moab, so they would come into Israel through the harvest season and intimidate the children of Israel into giving up the things that they worked for. And it's a shame but it's true. There are people who only come around during your harvest season. There are some people we will never hear from when we don't have anything. But let us be blessed with a little bit. Then all of a sudden they will come around and act like we talk every day. You don't believe me. Check your cell phone bill. Look at your text messages. Some folks only call you around the first of the month. If you are like me, some people only text you on the 15th or the 30th. You want to take it a step further. Get a promotion of your job. Better yet, hit the Mega Million or the Powerball. I guarantee you that you are going to get some phone calls from some people you never hear from. Because there are some people who are only interested in being around you in your harvest season. And let me take it a step further and say this. The people who show up in your harvest season are often the people who will discredit you if you don't deliver what they desire.

Don't fool yourself. There are some people who have a marauding spirit who will show up during your good times and try to latch on, fully prepared to take you down if you don't share what with them what God has given you.

That's why you have to careful who you allow in your space, when you see that God is blessing you. Be careful when you expanding your circle of friends that you don't allow someone in there who will burst the whole bubble. In other words, I am learning that I can trust people who were there when I didn't have anything more than I can trust some of those who want to be around me know that they think I got something! Don't try to be my friend now that I am a principal if you couldn't stand me when I was a teacher. Don't try to be my armor bearer now that I am a pastor when you used to walk out of the sanctuary when I first started preaching. Don't try to ask for a ride in my car now, when you wouldn't even stand next to me at the bus stop before. You see what I'm saying? If you weren't around when I struggled, don't try to get your hand on my harvest now!

Right there are some people right now who spoke death on my ministry…. Family… career. There were some people who did not believe I had what I took to be successful. They were whispering and talking behind the scenes. But juicy gossip always gets back to me. Don't kick my back in, and now try to ride my coat tails.

If you want to be blessed, don't try to snatch my harvest. Go tend your own fields. Go put your own work in. Leave what I have alone!

So, we have in the text, people with a Moabite mentality. People who will have a hand in your harvest. But then we have people who will sacrifice you to save themselves.

> *21 So it was, as they were burying a man, that suddenly they spied a band of raiders; and they cast the man in the tomb of Elisha;*

Don't miss it. These were supposed to be the people who cared about him. These were the people who were charged to make sure that the body was properly wrapped and laid in the tomb. The linens should have been in place. This man should have been given a proper burial. He should have been laid to rest with dignity. But because those carrying him were worried about what would happen to them if they were seen by the Moabites, they threw his body into the nearest grave and kept moving.

They placed him in somebody else's grave and kept moving. That is a great form of humility in the ancient text to have to be placed in somebody else's grave. It's the modern day equivalent of how some families never claim the body of a loved one because they don't want to pay for the funeral.

That's what we experience in the text. In the text, this dead man is left in another man's tomb because the people who cared about him chose their own wellbeing over ensuring that this man had a dignified death.

And the reality of life is that we live in a ME first world. We live in a world where people look out for themselves first. And oftentimes the result is that there are some who are discarded. Some who are cast out. This dead man in the text should have been shown some kindness. He should have given the decency of a burial, but in order to save themselves they throw him in another man's tomb.

And I hope that is a word for somebody today. Because there are people you are connected to, who will get rid of you to save themselves. There are people who will not have your back through everything.

Simply put: People have a ME-first mentality. Isn't that what happens John 5, the pool of Bethesda. Everybody at the pool has a problem? Lame. Withered. Diseased. Sick. Everybody is waiting at the pool, but when the water is troubled, nobody is trying to help that man get in the water, they are all trying to get in the water themselves.

People in this world are in it for themselves, and God needs somebody who is selfless enough to say that I am willing to help somebody even when I may need help myself!

And that is the message of the text. Because the text shows us that even in our sickness, faults, and frailties, what God has given us is still in us!

Don't miss the message. The Bible says,

> *21 And it came to pass, as they were burying a man, that, behold, they spied a band of men; and they cast the man into the sepulchre of Elisha: and when the man was let down , and touched the bones of Elisha, he revived , and stood up on his feet.*

Elisha is dead! And not just dead, but he is at the point of complete decomposition to where only his bones are left of his remains. But when the dead man's body is placed on his bones, he is revived and he stands on his feet! The ancient belief was that the bones of the dead retained at least for a while the supernatural power possessed by the deceased when he or she was alive.

Don't miss it! Elisha is dead. But he is still giving life! Because when you have been anointed by God, even in your dead state, you still have power.

At Elisha's weakest moment, he was able to revive the man! And this man was revived better than the last man. Why? Because in order for the boy in 2 Kings 4 to get up, Elisha had to lay on him twice. But this time, it only took Elisha touching him once. And this is where I want to close. Why was it harder for a healthy Elisha to resurrect the boy than it was for a dead Elisha to resurrect the man?

Because with the first resurrection, Elisha had not been through what they boy had been through, but with this second resurrection, Elisha was dead, but anointed. He had been through what the dead man had experienced!

And the best way to speak life to someone else is when you can identify with what I've been through. It's easy to tell me that God can deliver me from drugs, but it's more powerful when you can say I was a drug addict and God delivered me! It's easy to tell me that God can save me from an abusive relationship, but it's more powerful when you can say that I was abused and I made it out. It's easy to say that God can take care of me when I've lost my job, but it's more powerful when you can testify that you were unemployed and yet God made a way.

It's easy to tell me something, but when you've been through what I've gone through, that's when your words have power! And in this text, had Elisha not died, this man would not have lived. And so it is with Jesus, if Jesus had not died, we would not live!

It's Revival, And's It Necessary   Dr. Willie J. Thompson Jr.

2nd Kings 13:14-21

In studying Judaism, the question of human nature has always been of much debate. In this debate on the distinguishing characteristics, including the ways of thinking, feeling and acting, that humans tend to have naturally and independently of culture have been carefully examined to help us better understand why people do what they do make the choices they make and why people live the way they live. Now in Judaism there is a strong belief that Humanity was created in the "image" of the Creator. And the "image" of the Creator is the ability to discern and reason. Which means that Humanity has the inclination to both good and evil, and the Free Will is the ability to choose which inclination to follow.

If we ascribe to the thought of Judaism, all of us were created in the image of the Creator. We all were created to look like God, to be a reflection of God. In essence we were created to be a clone of God, God's twin, God's splitting Image and even God's stunt Double. If we ascribe to the thought of Judaism, if we are in his image, His image is the ability to discern and reason. God perceives, recognizes and detects. And God reflects, thinks and deliberates. And because we have these abilities despite the culture that we are surrounded by, we were made in the image of the Creator, we can think, reflect and detect and recognize, we have been given an inclination to both good and evil. Because we were made of God we have a natural proclivity, predilection and propensity to both Good and evil. And lastly, humanity was given an ability called "Free Will," and choose which urge we want to follow.

We are made in His image, given the ability to discern and reason, have the propensity to do both good and evil, and been given the free will to choose what urge or drive we want to follow.

We are like God, able to do God things, and yet are given a choice to do right or wrong and still be created in the image of God.

We can act Godly on Sunday, then wake up Monday and choose to live Godly or not. We can talk Godly on Sunday, then wake up on Monday and choose to talk God talk or not.

We can sell out to God on Sunday, and if we are not careful can be led away by an urge, an irritation, and distraction and a devil on Monday, and still be created in the image of God.

And the book of second kings is the perfect backdrop of what happens to people when they understand their human nature in the sciences but do not understand their human nature in God. If you don't understand that You are God's reflection, you will choose to misrepresent Him. If you don't understand that you are the works and hands of God, you will let critical situations miss their deliverance. If you don't understand that God has given you the ability to choose life and death, and wants you to choose life, you will miss the opportunity to fulfill your God given assignment. And it happens irregardless of where you came from. What neighborhood you grew up in. What schools you went to. What your last name is. What street you grew up on. What type of family you have come from. And what life you have built for yourself up to this point. You can miss it simply because of human nature.

And if you miss your opportunity, that which was meant to bring you life, will bring you death. If you miss your opportunity, that which was meant to bless you, will become a curse to you. If you mishandle the nature of God given to you, that which came to promote you will only come to torment you and buffet you. And overtake you in a way that even you will not be able to make your own choices. And this book of Kings is a perfect backdrop, because it is filled with people who mishandled the given nature of God, and very breath of God, the very neuma of God and found themselves in some tuff, challenging, disheartening, and today in some and dealing with some dead situations.

Two Kings, Jehoahaz and Jehoash are two examples of people who struggle with human nature, because in essence human nature gives you the options to go back and forth. It gives you the options to waver in between two opinions. And these two brothers are classic examples of what happens when you approach spiritual growth halfheartedly. When you are caught in between good and evil. You see, Jehoahaz cried out to God when he was in trouble, but as soon as God Brought relief, he went back and did what was evil in the sight of God. And I don't know if you know anybody like that, but, when they are in trouble, they run to God, but when everything is alright, they act like they don't know God. Don't judge them, it's human Nature.

> *Don't Judge Them.*
> *It's Human Nature.*

This second brother, Jehoash, has sort of the same problem, he wants to do his thing but has the nerve to cry out when Elisha was about to die. He was even there at Elisha's bedside at the time of death, and got instructions of what to do, but when he went to do it, he did it halfheartedly. You know half hearted, you do it, but you really don't feel it, so you do it just because. And I don't know if you know anybody like that, but these folks got one foot in the kingdom and one foot in the world. They want what God wants but they don't want to give God the control of the situation, so God can bring them out. You know halfheartedly, they bring it to the altar, but they put it in God's hands, part of the way. And you can't say it right now, but they, like this King of Israel are spiritless, uninterested, unenthusiastic and simply lukewarm. But God cannot do anything but tolerate people who will not make a complete commitment to God, and until you do that you are just as dead as you were before you heard God. In this hour you have got to commit and COME ALL THE WAY. If it looks good, and if it looks bad, COME ALL THE WAY. You might lose something and gain some things, but COME ALL THE WAY. You might have to change your walk and change your talk, but COME ALL THE WAY. You might put that down and pick that up, but don't waver in the middle. I know it's human nature. BUT YOU HAVE GOT TO COME ALL THE WAY. The bible says, Elijah yells out, "How long will you be caught in between two opinions? How long will you go limping in between two sides, if Jehovah is God, then serve Him" (1st Kings 18:21). They are both in trouble, dead, and find out that they need revival, because it is necessary.

Somebody wants to choose the good over the evil. Someone wants to choose life over death. Someone wants to choose, the blessings over the curses and sometimes the only way for that to happen, is For God TO BLOW His Breath back into you again and REVIVE YOU. It's Revival and It's Necessary.

The three characters in the text teach us a few distinct things: The raiders, the Israelites and the dead man all teach us something about the necessity of revival. We need revival because:

First the text teaches us, "The raiders will keep returning if you don't deal with them."

"The Moabites came every spring, to torment the Israelites."

The Moabites are enemies and enemies are persons or things that intend to oppress the interests of another. They constantly foster harmful designs against you and their sole purpose is to frustrate you to the point where you forget who God has called you to be. And the Moabites always had a way of showing up for Israel in the springtime. When things are just starting to grow. You know when things are really looking attractive and starting to bud and sprout. It is a transition time, you know it's not too hot and it's not too cold, things are just nice in the springtime. And for some reason Israel's enemies show up to plunder their stash and rain on their parade right in the moment of transition, right when you really are starting to get it together. They decide to come and crash your party. But the problem with this text is that the Moabites come around the same time not, once, not twice, not thrice, but every year they come and plunder all that you have been working hard all through the cold season to secure. We need revival because the raider must be dealt with. It is time to confront your enemies with the Word of God and the Power of God, because if not they will be back next year. They are not to be ignored, pushed under the carpet, or even closed up in the closet, they must be dealt with. And not just the external enemies, the one that always finds a way to hide in you: the ignorance, insecurities, selfishness, procrastination, lack of integrity, the exertion of your will on others and the disobedience and sin. They have been putting you on the run long enough. They have tormented you long enough. They have shut you down and halted from your destiny long enough. And if you don't deal with the enemies, they will be back next year, and with the same ole tricks from last year. But I came to inform somebody that when revival comes, it brings with it, the power to overcome our enemies and to finally get the guts to stand up and make

> *We need revival because the raider must be dealt with.*

70

the devil our footstool.

Not only is revival necessary so our enemies can be dealt with but the text also shares with us that revival is necessary because:

Some people's lives are going to have to be put in jeopardy before they let go or bury the dead things.

"When the Israelites saw the raiders coming, that's when they decided to let go of the dead thing."

Now, the raiders are people who attack an enemy on that enemy's territory or land. The Moabites were so bad, that they showed up at your house and beat you up, on your own lawn. They did not ask for an invitation, if they said they were going to get you at three o'clock, and you try to run and catch the bus and get home to where you thought you were safe, they would show up at your house and beat you up and take your stuff in front of your screaming momma, Saying Leave, my child alone. The Moabites were the tough kids on the block. And when the Israelites saw from afar off the raiders coming, they decided to drop the dead thing and run for their lives. And if the truth be told again, some of us will not let the dead thing go and stop holding on to that dead thing until our lives are put in jeopardy. We will not let go of the anger and unforgiveness, until the doctor says, it's killing you. We will not let go of that bad relationship until it brings us home a life threatening disease. We will not let that gossip go until it is the truth about our child. We will not let racist, classist and sexist attitudes go until our lives are put in jeopardy. We sometimes will not stop excessive smoking, drinking and drug use, until the day our mother needs a kidney and we have none to give. Our nurse needs a vein and we have none that can be found. And our children need chemotherapy, because they have suffered from 2nd hand smoke between conception and age 5. And these folk saw their lives, and they saw the dead thing they were holding on to, and the dead thing they were dealing with and decided to throw that joker in the tomb and run for your life!

> *Don't you know, dead things will let you carry them as long as you want too.*

Dead things will not just go away; you have to make up your mind to do something about it.

Not only is revival necessary so our enemies can be dealt, and revival is necessary because some people's lives will have to be put in jeopardy, before they let go of Dead things, with but the text also shares with us that revival is necessary because:

Some things are going to have to be discarded before they are revived.

"They threw him in the grave of Elisha, and when he touched Elisha's bones he revived."

And sometimes it is not until you are left for dead, that you become a prime candidate for revival. Sometimes it is not until you have been written off and cast aside that you become a candidate for a divine revival. Sometimes it is not until you have been so badly damaged by that situation, that you become a prime candidate for a come around. Sometimes it is not until you have been neglected, that you become a candidate to be accepted. Sometimes it is not until you have been abandoned by all that you know, that you become a candidate to be renovated and repaired. Sometimes it is not until you have been cast-off, that you become a candidate for real consolation. Sometimes it is not until people say they are done with you that you become a candidate for the people who really will help you. Sometimes it is not until you have been thrown out that you become a candidate to walk into what will never throw you out. Sometimes it is not until you are out of date that you become a candidate to be restarted and revised. Sometimes it is not until you have been run down that you become a candidate to snap out of it and move on with your life. Sometimes it is not until you have been thrown away that you become a candidate to be recycled. Sometimes it is not until you have been junked and cast away that you become a candidate for a touch up, a spring up and wake up.

They threw this brother in the grave. But, when he was thrown in the grave, the grave was filled with the bones of a man that still had power to bring you back to life. So let them throw you away. Let them cast you aside. Let them leave you for dead. If they leave you, the Lord will pick you up. If they walk out on you, the Lord will take care of you. Throw me away, God will pick me Up. Leave me for dead, God will bring me back. Put me off on somebody else, God will bring me back better than ever.

But wait a minute. In Israelite culture the denial or proper burial to a man or to toss his body into a common pit of corpses indicated the greatest disgrace heaped upon the reputation of the deceased and their family (Isaiah 14:18-20). In essence, to toss someone in someone else's tomb or to toss him in a place where the dead were, was a bold statement against the reputation of the dead. You know how people act, if you don't put away your loved one in something nice. It said, this person did not even have the common sense of life to prepare for their own burial. Because everybody that lives is surely going to die. And it only makes sense to prepare yourself for death. So to be tossed in someone else's grave speaks to the your reputation and the reputation of your family.

But there is something going on behind the text. Don't you remember that in this book the law of sowing and reaping is in effect. A theology of retribution is the scarlet thread in the pericope. Meaning you can't sow without reaping and no seed comes forth out of the ground, unless it dies first.

Don't you know that every person is the seed of Abraham. So this brother had to come back to life, because you can't cast a seed into the ground without it coming back to life. Jesus says in John 12:24, *"unless a seed falls into the ground and die, it can not be brought back to life."* And some things can't come back until they die. Tell somebody, just let it die.

They threw him in another man's grave and tomb, and the bible says "he revived, jumped up and walked out on his own two feet." And this brother was not the only one (seed) who was cast into another man's grave and had the nerve to get back up and walk out of his own accord.

They tell me that after another brother, first John 3:19, calls him the "Only Begotten of God and the Divine Seed," forgave two thieves on his left and right. After, another brother, a Divine Seed, made sure his mother had a plan for security upon his departure. Another brother cried out "why has thou forsaken me?" After another brother said, "Into thine hands I commend my spirit." After another brother, a Divine Seed, cried out "It is finished," and gave up the ghost. After another brother died until people cried out "surely this was the son of God. After another brother died and caused the moon and the sun to refuse to shine. After another died, and was taken from the cross by a man named Joseph of Armithea, who was helped by Nicodemus. A dead man, a Divine Seed, named Jesus.

The word was out, it was over, Jesus was finally gone. They posted it in the courier, the Washington Post, the New York Times and in every town, Jesus was dead. And they took the dead man named Jesus, a Divine Seed, and laid him in somebody else's tomb. And when they did this, they put his name in question. When they did this they put his reputation on the line.

And God remembered 2nd Kings 13:21, and thought to himself, Jesus has got to come back. Because My Name is on the line, my reputation is on the line, my word is on the line. And I promised my people, that "God is not a man that he should lie nor the Son of Man that he should repent. If God said it, He is gonna do it, if God spoke it, God will surely bring it to past. Jesus had to come back because he was the Seed of God being planted in the ground. But in another man's tomb. And the word says, Do not Be Deceived, God is not mocked, whatsoever a man sows, that so shall he reap. He had to bring Jesus back, because you can't put the Seed in the ground, and the seed not revive, get up and walk out on its own accord.

> *You can't put the Seed in the ground, and the seed not revive, get up and walk out on its own accord.*

And somebody in this room has been tossed aside and messed around and landed in a borrowed tomb. But if you land and stay in a borrowed tomb, you tarnish the reputation of your heavenly father, and before God allows his reputation to be destroyed, messed up or tarnished, though you were considered and left for dead. God will bring you back. It's not that you have been so good, but it's the critical fact that the reputation of God is at stake. And before, His name is tarnished. He will bring even you, with your dead self, back. His name is on the line so you have to be revived. His word is at stake, so you have to make a comeback. His laws are being questioned, so you have got to come back to life. And when you get revived, have enough sense to jump-up and walk out on your own accord. It's Revival. And it's necessary, because God's Name is on the Line.

-FOUR-

Jesus resurrects the widow's son at Nain

Luke 7:13-15 (KJV)

13 And when the Lord saw her, he had compassion on her, and said unto her, Weep not.

14 And he came and touched the bier: and they that bare him stood still. And he said, Young man, I say unto thee, Arise.

15 And he that was dead sat up, and began to speak. And he delivered him to his mother.

I Matter to God   Rev. John H. Gamble Jr.

Jesus and the Widow of Nain

Luke 7:11-17

An old man was walking the beach. As the sun rises, the indicator that a new day has dawned, he noticed a young man ahead of him picking up starfish and flinging them into the sea. Eventually the old man caught up with the young man to ask him what he was doing. The young man replied that he was he was throwing the starfish back into the water, because the stranded starfish would die if they were left in the morning sun.

The old man looked at the boy and said, "But the beach goes on for miles and miles, and there are millions of starfish. How is what you are doing going to make any difference?"

The young man looked at the starfish in his hand, threw it to safety of the water. And he said to the old man, "It makes a difference to this one."

This old man walked the beach daily. But yet, he didn't even notice the starfish until he saw the young man throwing the starfish. He was caught up on the beauty of the sun rising over the horizon, that he missed an opportunity to save the starfish lives. Because the sunrise was what everyone came to see. The sunrise was significant. No one wanted to pay attention to some starfish that were washed ashore by currents they couldn't control. The beauty of the sunrise made the starfish insignificant to those who walked the boast. But each morning, there were starfish that were saved from certain death because they mattered to the young man.

And let me caution us, children of God, to be careful not to invest our time and attention in the wrong place. (Because) If truth be told, some of us have been guilty of the mindset of this miserly, old man. We place a premium on the people, places, and things that we find important, and as a result we can miss out on the people, places, and things that really could need our help.

And let me suggest that this is the tension of the text. Because in Luke 7, Jesus performed two miracles. One in a major seaport called Capernaum, the other in a small city called Nain. You know the story. A roman official, called a centurion, has a servant who is sick and about to die. He hears that Jesus is passing by. He sends the Jewish leaders to Jesus to request that Jesus comes to his house to heal the servant. And if you read chapter 7, verses 4 and 5, it says that they go to Jesus and begs him to come saying, "This man deserves to have you do this, because he loves our nation and has built our synagogue." In other words, they are saying to Jesus. "This man is too important to not pay attention to his request." They go to Jesus because of this man's status. The centurion had a direction connection to the Roman governors, who reported directly to the Roman emperor or king. In other words, they wanted Jesus to go to this man's house because of who he was connected to. But they didn't realize that this man's connection didn't matter to Jesus, who is the King of Kings. He did not need this man's approval or authority to validate his ministry. Jesus is one his way to the house not because of the political status of the centurion, but he is on his way because of the personal affliction of the centurion's servant.

You see if you read the text, the centurion understands his place. He gets it. When Jesus gets close to the house, he sends a message to Jesus saying, "Lord, do not trouble yourself, for I am not worthy that You should enter under my roof. But please just say the word, and my servant will be healed. I have authority over soldier. If I tell them to go, they go. If I tell them to come, they come. But my authority pales in comparison to your authority." And after hearing this Roman soldier express authentic faith, Jesus heals without ever making a house visit.

But here is where we need to place the crux of the conversation. The text says,

> *11 Now it happened, the day after, that He went into a city called Nain; and many of His disciples went with Him, and a large crowd. 12 And when He came near the gate of the city, behold, a dead man was being carried out, the only son of his mother; and she was a widow. And a large crowd from the city was with her.*

Don't miss it. The centurion's servant was sick, and had progressed to the point of death. The next day, Jesus walks into a city and encounters a funeral procession of a young man who was sick and died. The proximity of the events would suggest that the centurion's servant and the woman's son were sick at the same time. But the one who gets the immediate benefit, the one who gets the message to Jesus is the one who lives in the big city, and has the big title. It's the status of the centurion that gets the message to Jesus, whereas the greater need was for this young man, this son of this widowed woman to be healed. Don't miss the text. She was a widow. This was her only son. She has already buried her husband, but now she has to bury her only son. With the death of the men in her life, she has no one available to care for her and she is left to the mercy of a society that will not be fully invested in her wellbeing. Don't miss it. The centurion can get another servant, but the woman can't get another son. Yet she is placed low priority, because of who she is and where she lives.

The centurion lived in Capernaum. Capernaum is less than twenty five miles from Nain, which means that the message of her son's illness could have been relayed to Jesus. Jesus could have come to Nain first, preventing his death in the first place. But because she is in Nain, there is no message sent to the master. The attention is given to the industrial city, and not the insignificant city.

Capernaum was the major fishing port. Capernaum was the place where the money was made so it seems like Capernaum gets more attention. And sometimes in life, attention is given to the people, places, and things that don't need it, and the ones who need it the most suffer because there is no one there to help those who really need ministry. Peter's mother in law is healed on her fever in Capernaum. The man sick of the palsy is lowered through the roof and healed in Capernaum. There is a man with an unclean spirit healed in Capernaum. Capernaum is a major city, with major resources and it seems like Capernaum dominates Jesus' attention. Jesus seems to constantly be kept in Capernaum, when there are some folks in Nain who need to be connected with the Lord.

Nain only shows up in scripture one time. AND this is it! Nain doesn't get attention like the other cities. No one talks about Nain. The only information that appears about Nain is that it was a beautiful place. But I am sure Nain had issues in the city like any other city. But because the city was not sizable or significant. It was ignored.

Here is the message. We have to be careful how we assess where people are in their lives because sometimes their identity does not match their reality. It's implicit in the text. People in scripture are identified by the town from which they come. Jesus of Nazareth. Simon of Syrene. Joseph of Arimithea. You were identified with the place. However, your identity does not always align with your reality. Identity is determined by location. Reality is determined by situation. Nain is translated Pleasure, Beauty, and Green Pastures. That was her identity. But her reality is that she is experiencing Panic, Burden, and Grief-Stricken Pain. By location, she should have everything she needs, but her situation says that when her son dies, it's going to be difficult to live. She is not going to see her way through. She will be at a moment of stress and strain as she leads the funeral procession to bury her son. And let me tell you that whenever you identity and your reality are not aligned, whenever your location is in contradiction to your situation, you are going to feel stress and strain in your life.

Let me see if I can help you. There is not more difficult that to come to church when somebody in the church has gotten on your nerves. Why? Because we identify the church as the house of worship…. The place for our breakthrough…. Where we get to hear a word from the Lord. But because our situation – somebody has gotten on our nerves- does not match our situation, it becomes harder to worship. You have to move your seat to focus. You start visiting other church. You start skipping worship. You don't talk to people like you used to. That's because you have allowed the stress and the strain that comes with dis-alignment to affect your ability to worship freely.

The reality is who you are will never always match what you are going through. But if you get through what you are going through, God has the potential to build on it to make you a new you!

This woman loses her son, when if she had access to Jesus the way the centurion gained access to Jesus, her son would not have died. But look at the text; it says the next day, Jesus went into a city called Nain. His disciples went with Him. A large crowd is following him and as they were walking in, a funeral procession is coming out. Now, here's what excites me about the text. Nain is only mentioned in the Scripture once. No one sends word to Jesus about this son's sickness. There is no obituary announcement. Yet Jesus shows up!

We don't know what to shout about. Graves were usually placed on the outside of the city. The funeral procession to the grave would start with the mother of the deceased walking in front, her close family members behind her. Then the body, in a cedar coffin was carried on a bier. After the coffin, the relatives, friends, and mourners followed. They processed to the gravesite. Jewish cemeteries were outside the city wall in order to avoid pollution by dead corpses. And so, in the text, they get to the gate of the city and before they can turn toward the cemetery, Jesus is there! And that's a message for somebody today. Just because we may feel that God is not there when we first experience our pain; that does not mean that God will not show up! He will show up! Don't miss it. Jesus met them at the gate. The gates of the city were designed to provide protection against wild animals, criminals, and foreign armies. In other words, this woman was in enough pain at the loss of her son, but once she left the gates of the city, she and the whole funeral procession, would be vulnerable to the attack of wild animals and criminals that could try to steal or kill what little she had left. Jesus shows up at the gates of the city, and raises her son. And as a result, she never has to experience what could take place from the city gate to the cemetery. And that ought to encourage somebody today. You matter to God so much that while he does not exempt you from everything, he will show up and keep you from going from bad to worse. I dare you to look back at your life. Some of us can be honest and say we have been through some pretty messed up situations…. Foolishness… hard times… stress and some strain in our lives, and if it had not been for God covering us, it would have been much worse than what it is! If you don't believe that God has shown up at your gates, I dare you to look back at that accident that almost left you paralyzed, that gun shot that almost took your life, that sickness that almost took you out of here. There are some situations in life that God did not exempt you from, but he showed up before things went from bad to worse! Thank God that he knows how much I can bear!

Look at this woman. She is a widow. She has lost her husband and her only son. Her support system seems to be gone. Yes, there is a large crowd following her. But they are only there because her son died. We know how it goes. Everyone comes to the funeral, so they can experience the repast. They are there. They are at the service. But when they leave, she is going to be left on her own. I am sure this woman does not know what her future will be, but Jesus shows up and she learns a lesson from the Lord. And that's really the message today. The sermon is simple. Because you matter to God, things are never as bad as they seem. (That should encourage someone today.)

And that's what we see in the text. The Bible says,

> *11 Now it happened, the day after, that He went into a city called Nain; and many of His disciples went with Him, and a large crowd. 12 And when He came near the gate of the city, behold, a dead man was being carried out, the only son of his mother; and she was a widow. And a large crowd from the city was with her.*

Remember that I told you that the distance from Capernaum to Nain is 20 to 25 miles. If you Google it, it is a 43 minute ride driving today. (The distance from New York to New Brunswick). There was no boat to get there. He couldn't cross over the sea. The only way to get there was to walk. But the Bible says that he healed the centurion's servant, and the next day he started walking to Nain. And let's not kid ourselves. It seems like a far walk. For us, it would be like getting on the Turnpike at exit 14 and walking to exit 8. Or getting on the Parkway at South Orange Avenue exit 143 and walking to exit 100 which is the exit for Freehold.

But it seems far because we are used to getting in our car and going. But for Jesus this was a difficult journey, but a doable journey. It was less than 25 miles. If he started walking in the morning, he would be there by the evening. In other words, he was incredibly close. And that's what we need to remember, no matter how far it seems God is away from us, God can always get to us! God is IMMANENTLY CLOSE!

And that is important because people want to paint a picture of an impersonal God. They want us to see a God that is not interested or involved in the affairs of man. But that's not what I see in scripture. I see a God who did not just the Creator, but we serve a God who is involved in what he created! You don't believe me. Ask Moses (Exodus 3 – Burning bush). You don't think he is present. Ask the children of Israel who are led by a

> *I see a God who did not just the Creator, but we serve a God who is involved in what he created!*

cloud in the day and a pillar of fire in the night. You don't think he is present. Ask Elijah would stood on the side of the mountain, with 450 false prophets on the other, and watched as fire from heaven consumed the sacrifice, the altar, and the water around the altar. If you don't think God will show up. Ask Elisha's servant, who was afraid of the Aramean armies. When God opened his eyes. He saw the Aramean armies, but he also saw them surrounded by an army with chariots of fire.

God is incredibly close. It is called the immanency of God. God is present in creation! That's why "David" in Psalm 139 raised the question, "Where can I go from your Spirit? Where can I flee from your presence?...."

God is immanent. He is active and present in the world! HE has not forsaken the world. He still has the whole world in His hand.

But not only is his presence immanent (SPELL IT), but his promise is imminent (SPELL THAT), meaning he has the absolute ability to deliver on what he says. Let me put it like this. In our Christian clichés, we often say, "God said it. I believe it. That settles it." But the truth is if God says it, it does not matter whether we believe or not, it shall come to pass.

Isn't that what happens in the first 10 verses? The centurion came to Jesus in faith, believing that Jesus could heal his servant. Jesus said, "I have not found such great faith, not even in Israel." And when you read the story in Matthew 8, it says that Jesus said, "Go! Let it be done just as you believed it would." And his servant was healed at that moment.

Because God's promises are imminent! If he said it, it will come to pass, according to your faith. That's why we need to know and believe that God has greater for us than where we are right now. We have to believe that God can do even more for us and with us than what he has already done. Because if we ask for God, and God approves it, it is an absolute guarantee we shall receive it!

We matter to God, and because we matter to God, God stays incredibly close.

> ## God doesn't get too far away from us!

He is immanently close, but then he is Indiscriminately Concerned. The text says,

> *13 When the Lord saw her, He had compassion on her and said to her, "Do not weep."*

This one is not deep. Let me put it right where we can get it. Some people never care, but GOD cares. Some people will never have your best interest at heart, but God will always look out for us. Let me say this.

Just because people exhibit the same emotion as you, doesn't mean that they care about you. Remember in the funeral procession, the mother leads out the body. The body is then followed by relatives, friends, and mourners. When you understand the role of the mourners, you will get the meat of this point in the message.

The funeral procession was a dramatic event. There was a large crowd. The cries and tears are loud and piercing. People are joining the parade out of the city, because there are so many people who are crying and their grief seems to be of the same magnitude of this mother who has lost her son. However, what is missing from the text is that the true mourners were the mother, the family, and the friends. But then there were professional mourners. There were people in the processional who were paid to cry. They appeared to be in bereavement. They appear to be concerned. But the minute they stop receiving pay, when then check was cut at the end of the processional, their tears dry up. They get off the line and they are on to the next job. Because they only cry like the mother cries when it stands to benefit them. And there are some people in your life that are only around for what it benefits them. Some of us have friends who are really nothing but hired mourners. Some of us have connections that are nothing but hired mourners. And As soon as your status changes, they are going to unfriend you! The minute your condition changes they are going to be nowhere to be found. But compassion for them is connected to compensation, and it's not the crux of their character.

This isn't too hard to get. Everyone that comes to a funeral is not coming to pay respect to the dead. Some folks show up to the funeral to make sure the person is dead. Some do not show up to help the family. Some people skip the funeral and are the first people sitting at the table for the repast. Some people come to the funeral so they can get the inside track on when the family is going to get rid of the possessions of the deceased so they can get some free stuff under the cover of "I want something to remember him/her by." There are some hired mourners in our lives who could care less about what we are going through. But that's not how Jesus is! How do I know? Because the same compassion he had for the centurion in the first 10 verses is the same compassion he had for this mother in the next 6 to 7 verses! Her singleness didn't matter…. Loneliness…. Brokenness… impending poverty was irrelevant. Jesus cared!

Patrick, the two-day-old son of President John F. Kennedy, was fighting for his life because of a lung condition. The President went to see him on the hospital's fifth floor, which had been cleared of all visitors.

On his way to the room, President Kennedy passed by an open door and saw two girls, three or four years old, playing in bed. They were both terribly burned and bandaged.

Kennedy learned one of the children would probably lose one of her hands. The president wrote a note to each girl. After several minutes he went to his own son's room. Patrick died the next day.

If the president can show love and concern to two unknown children while his own son is suffering and dying, how much more will God show concern for us!

That's why Peter could write in 1 Peter 5:7, "Cast your cares on the LORD and he will sustain you; he will never let the righteous be shaken. He will never let the God slip and fall!"

Let me help someone in here today and tell somebody Jesus cares. He cares about you. Other people may come to see you fall…. Witness your destruction… see you down and out. But God is committed to your growth…. Prosperity… wellbeing… God's wants you positive, productive, and promoted. God wants you educated, elevated, and consecrated. God wants you doing well, feeling well, and living well.

You are more valuable than the sparrows. The hairs on your very head are numbered. GOD CARES ABOUT YOU!

You matter to God. And because you matter God stays immanently close. He is indiscriminately concerned, but then he has an Incredible Touch. Notice the text. The Bible says,

> *14 Then He came and touched the open coffin, and those who carried him stood still. And He said, "Young man, I say to you, arise." 15 So he who was dead sat up and began to speak. And He presented him to his mother.*

Now, one of the unique aspects of this miracle is that Jesus when Jesus heals, he normally heals by touching or being touched. The man who was born blind, Jesus touched him. The woman with the issue of blood was touched by Jesus. However, in this miracle, Jesus does not touch the dead man, nor can the dead man touch him, and yet the man is still healed. Number 19:11 says that if a man comes in contact with a dead body, he was defiled, and to be considered unclean for seven days.

Jesus shows up at the funeral procession and he does not touch the body, but he touches the bier. He touches the coffin on which the man is laid. And the bible says, not only does the boy raise up, but he immediately begins to speak!

We are missing it! We are used to asking God to touch us! We want God's hands on us. We agree with Isaiah when he said, "All of us have become like one who is unclean, and all our righteous acts are like filthy rags. You have hidden your face from us and have given us over to our sins. Yet you, LORD, are our Father. We are the clay, you are the potter; we are all the work of your hands."

We want to be in God's hands. We want God to touch us. But the truth is God can bless us even when he is not touching us. But he is touching the things around us!

God doesn't have to touch you. He can change your life by touching the things around you. He doesn't have to touch you, but you can be blessed if He touches the people you hang around with.

- He doesn't have to touch you, but you can be blessed if He touches the bus driver or the train conductor with the skills they need to get you to work safely every morning

> *God doesn't have to touch you. He can change your life by touching the things around you.*

- He doesn't have to touch you, but you can be blessed if He touches the doctor with the wisdom and insight he needs before he performs your surgery

- He doesn't have to touch you, but you can be blessed if He touches the person who has access to the HR department that just looked at your resume for the job of your dreams.

It doesn't matter if God doesn't touch you, you can be blessed when He starts the things around you!

That's why You ought to praise God, not just when he touches you, but when he touches the things around you.

You ought to praise God, not just when he touches you, but when he touches the people around you. That's why I learned not just to pray for myself, but to for the people I am connected to. Because when God touches them, I receive an indirect investment deposit into my life from the Lord.

Look at your neighbor and say, "Neighbor, I am praying that God touches you." You see, if I pray that God touches the people around me, and you pray that God touches the people around you, it is not long before we have all be touched by the Lord!

We ought to praise God! Not just when he touches us, but when He touches the things around us!

When Revival Shows Up   Dr. Willie J. Thompson Jr.

Luke 7:11-17 (The Message Bible)

11-15 Not long after that, Jesus went to the village Nain. His disciples were with him, along with quite a large crowd. As they approached the village gate, they met a funeral procession—a woman's only son was being carried out for burial. And the mother was a widow. When Jesus saw her, his heart broke. He said to her, "Don't cry." Then he went over and touched the coffin. The pallbearers stopped. He said, "Young man, I tell you: Get up." The dead son sat up and began talking. Jesus presented him to his mother. 16-17 They all realized they were in a place of holy mystery, that God was at work among them. They were quietly worshipful—and then noisily grateful, calling out among themselves, "God is back, looking to the needs of his people!" The news of Jesus spread all through the country.

When Revival Shows Up.

There are over 3.7 million Christian congregations in the world according to the Institute on Religion and Research. There are 3.7 million spaces on this earth where people can have fellowship with the crucified and risen Christ. To be forgiven, to hear the voices of God. To grow in the knowledge of the Bible, God's Word. To feed your soul, to be loved and encouraged, to be prayed for, to love and encourage your fellow Christian believers; to worship and to promote the Gospel.

On earth there are 3.7 million churches, and if that's true, for the 6 billion people in the world, a church must be and should be nearby. According to reddit.com, there are more churches in the United States than convenience stores, fast food restaurants, hotels, and motels combined.

450,000 places where people come together and deal with and do the business of God.

There are 2900 miles distance between New York and San Francisco, and if there are 450,00 churches, if you drove straight across you would be in a one miles radius of at least 64 sanctuaries, filled with people who name the name of Christ as Savior and declare Jesus as Lord for every one mile you drove. They are everywhere, and come in all shapes and sizes. Baptist, Methodist, Pentecostal, Catholic, COGIC, non-denominational, Presbyterian, interdenominational, and ecumenical.

And in them, you can have fellowship with the crucified and risen savior. In them you can be forgiven and hear the word of God. In them you can learn more about the Bible and feed your soul. And if you can find it anywhere else if you make it to one of these 450,000 churches or even 21 churches in Clairton, PA, you can at least find encouragement, love, be prayed for and have the opportunity to pray for somebody else. And it is happening at least 64 times for every mile you drive or walk or run in this country.

But where do you go when there is no church? Where do you get your encouragement from when there is no church? How do you learn about Gods word the bible when there is no church? How do you feed your spirit and your soul when there is no church?

> *But where do you go when there is no church?*

This question becomes important today, because in our text the story of today's pericope is set in a little suburb town called Nain. And Nain is a small town also known as a hamlet, which is a small village that has no church of its own. Have you ever been to a town that has no church? We can find a church on every corner, near most red dot stores in mostly every community. But where do you go for help when you need it and there is no church.

Nain is the setting of today's text, for it was a small town, but filled with people and had no church. They might have had buildings, but no church; they might have had businesses, convenience stores, little motels, but no church. I don't know about you, but in most of the little towns I've been to, there was always a church. Where was the church in Nain? Where did the people go for weddings, and Sunday services, where did the people go for encouragement, and to be forgiven and to be prayed for.

Wait, in the text, a large crowd of people are coming from a funeral on the way to the graveyard to bury a young man. It must be a church in Nain. Where did they just have the service, were they outside under the sky and now on the way to the cemetery, where did they have the service? It must be a church there! The people were religious, I think. Because they came to the service, but where did they get their understanding from, how did they know to show up, how did they know to weep with those who weep and mourn with those who mourn. And if everything was all-good why did Jesus have to interrupt the funeral recessional.

Let's push this, maybe it is some buildings, in Nain, with crosses on them but they were not the church. Maybe there were some places and places with the Torah on the platform, but they were not churches. Maybe they had buildings where people gathered and talked more about themselves and nothing about God. There were no churches in Nain. Maybe they had groups of people who came together to promote each other, especially those who had a little cheese and green, but never took time to help those who had nothing,.. There were no churches in Nain. Maybe they had buildings where people came to see men and women dressed in holy garments, but lived ratchet lifestyles. Maybe they had buildings that had special seating for the rich, and special seats at the table for the noblest of society. Maybe they had spaces that were committed to the dead and usable to the living. THERE were no churches in Nain. Maybe they had buildings filled with people who came to argue the bible and not believe the Bible, maybe they had spots and places where people could go to meet up with each other and forget to meet up with God. THERE were no churches in Nain.

And here in our text a large group of people are doing a religious service and Jesus shows up and interrupts and brings revival because, whenever Jesus shows up, God's church can be erected in the lives of his people.

They are on the way to the final resting place of the dead but when Jesus shows up and brings revival to a dead situation, things turn around and Nain the city would have no town, becomes a town, who not only have buildings but living stones. And living epistles and living witnesses to the power of God in their lives.

If we look carefully at the text, I believe there are three things, we can't extract that causes revival to show up.

> *Revival shows up, when resources run out!*

The woman in the text has lost her husband and her son. This widow is in the same position as Naomi in the book of Ruth, husband and son are gone. She has no one to care for her. No one to provide for her and Jesus knows the despair and the embarrassment that comes along to persons who have to seek alms from a church-less small town. She had no options, because the people for years have had no religious service but not relationship with God. She was out of resources. She had no support, supply or aid that she could draw upon when she needed. If she had her husband and lost her son it would be different. And if she lost her husband and had her son it would be different. But what happens when both rivers run dry? What do you do when you have placed your eggs in multiple baskets, and still end up losing it all? What did you do when 401k plans plummeted and the bottom dropped out of the housing market? What do you do when you lose two vital resources at the same time? Jesus saw her and had compassion on her because he knew that when resources run out, you become a prime candidate for a God In Christ encounter and The bible says Jesus felt for her and Revival Showed Up!

I would like to suggest secondly that Revival does not come until Crowd Comforts are Considered Concrete:

In our text, the Bible records that the procession was headed to the cemetery, to the final resting place of the dead and a large crowd followed this woman as she wept and cried for her son. It seemed like they were going to go with her all the way to the end. In this text one fourth of the people decided not to go to the fellowship hall and wait for the family to return. In this text, one fourth of the people decided not to just come to the service and get an obituary. In this text one fourth of the people decided to not just come and view the body, to see how well "Waters," did, but the majority, and the Bibles describes them a large crowd was going with the sister all the way to the end. And may I suggest that revival may not show up until crowd comforts seem concrete. You have to be careful with the crowd, because sometimes the crowd can give you a false sense of hope that will not last. Rick Warren, in his book called "The Purpose Driven Church," describes the crowd as regular attenders, they sometimes cannot be depended on as a core team player, but they do show up on a regular basis, to sometimes make the point that they came. You have to be careful of the crowd, because the crowd can convince you that they are in it for the long haul. You see, the crowd has the ability to show up, because something good is going on, but after that which was going on is over, the crowd disperses and the committed hang around to get the job done. This woman had a large crowd with her and it seemed like their support was concrete. It seems like they were with her until the end, but don't you know that everyone who comes to the party doesn't stay around to help you clean up. You have to be careful of the crowd, because the crowd will support you today and then when times get hard, they will be nowhere to be found. You have to be careful of the crowd because today they will shout your praises and tomorrow, they will yell out crucify you. And Jesus shows up on the scene and knows that the crowd will follow you as long as you are providing something, and that's not bad, but the minute the dish changes the crowd will go back to their corners until something good happens. And for this one woman, it seems that the crowd's comfort was concrete, it looked like they had her back, she was a widow and now she was childless, and Jesus shows up and the Bible says he felt sorry for her. And told her not to weep. I would like to suggest that He knew all too well that the crowds are not the committed. And one day you can feed five thousand and the next day you can be down to 11, so he shows up to let her and us know, don't be tricked by the crowd, it provides a level of comfort, but it ain't concrete.

The Bibles says the woman who was a widow and lost her only son was in the procession with a very large crowd, they were on their way to the burial ground and Jesus shows up also with a crowd, and the Bibles says He had compassion on her. His said to this woman, who is at the point of pain so extensive that she is weeping, so loudly that Jesus can hear her over the crowd with him and the crowd with her. There are no other details given in the text, it does not say who she was or what was her status. It did not say where she worked or how the son and the husband die. The story does not tell us, how the sermon was or if they brought cards and gifts to comfort her. But it does tell us she was weeping and Jesus told her to stop. And the text calls this compassion. Normally people would say to extend compassion is to feel sorry or to have empathy, or to just be there in the time of trouble. But Jesus takes this compassion thing to a whole nother level. He not only shows up, but he also does something about the situation.

Lastly, I would like to suggest that revival might not come until Christ's compassion can be conveyed.

Jesus shows up and interrupts the procession and tells this mother not to cry; tells the pallbearers to stop; places his finger on the bier; and tells the young man to get up. Excuse me sir, who do you think you are, interrupting this funeral, not permitting this woman not to cry, stopping the pallbearers who may be carrying a heavy bier. Excuse me sir, don't you know we have to be at the cemetery by a certain hour or they will charge us more. Excuse me sir, don't you see we have to get this crowd of people back to the church and get them some fried chicken and green beans. And here you are interrupting the funeral procession. Who do you think you are? And Jesus tells the boy to get up and the boy gets up. I believe it is more than a resurrection here in the text, but Christ may be trying to help us understand that, to have compassion, is not to just show up, it's a part of it, but not all of it. Jesus may be trying to help us understand that dropping of a cake or two and coming to the service is a part of it, but it is not all of it. But maybe Jesus wants us to catch a new understanding of compassion, it's not just knowing about it, He conveys to us to do something about it. He saw her and had compassion on her and went into action. And maybe Jesus wants us to not only know about the homeless, locate the homeless, but maybe he wants us to get up and build something that those who encounter homelessness, can have a place to get back on their feet. Maybe Jesus wants us to not only know the sick and in need of healing, but maybe Jesus wants you to get up and go by and lay hands on the sick and watch them recover right before their eyes. Maybe revival does not come until Christ can convey compassion. Revival shows up when our understanding of compassion is activated. It's not just to know it, it's to fix it. It's not just to acknowledge it, it's to turn it around. It's not just to point it out, it's to pick it up. Revivals show up when we get up and change some things. It's when compassion is put in action. It's when you do something about what you see. That's when revival shows up.

> *Revival shows up when our understanding of compassion is activated.*

Jesus interrupts the journey to do something about this woman's situation. Jesus stops a boy from going to his final resting place just so he can extend some compassion. And he calls the boy back to life. He does something, he shows some mercy, he extends some grace and he expresses some kindness. She didn't ask for it, she just got it. She did not qualify, but the resurrection and the life was at her side. But here Jesus interrupts the funeral to give a woman her son back. He assures that she is now given back what she needs to carry on after the crowd has dispersed. She had no one to look after her once this was over, and because of this, Jesus stopped the procession to give her back a resource of sustainability because he knew the crowd comfort was not concrete. He knew that when resources run dry, life will get tough, so he gives this woman her back.

Doesn't that sound familiar? Jesus interrupts certain processes just so he can make sure a widow has a son to take care of her for the rest of her days. Doesn't that sound familiar? Jesus disturbing certain events, just so he can make sure that a woman who could even get a seat in the revival one night, because of the crowd, would have some help when she got old. Doesn't that sound familiar? Jesus holding up certain events, just to make sure a woman who was crying at the foot of the cross, with at least 21 roman soldiers all around looking on her pain. Doesn't that sound familiar? Jesus suspending and delaying certain events, just to make sure that a woman, who had lost her husband and her son, was given something to make sure she had a meal and a place to lay her head.

Don't you despise the interruptions? Jesus interrupted the process of crucifixion, just so he could make sure that Mary could experience revival. He told the blood that was rushing to his head, HOLD ON; I have got to do something. He told the rusty nails in his hand, HOLD ON, I've got to do something. He told his unquenchable thirst, HOLD ON, I've got to do something. He told the crown of thorns that had been pressed into his head that would normally cause hallucinations, to HOLD ON; I've got to do something. He told the nails in his feet, you may be stopping me from walking but HOLD ON, I've got to do something. Jesus interrupts the process of crucifixion and death. Jesus looks over at his mother, who was a widow and now about to lose her first-born son. And has compassion on her, and says, Woman Behold thy son, and Son behold thy mother. Jesus interrupted death, just so he could convey compassion. And that's when revival shows up. It shows up when compassion is put in action, even if it interrupts what's already going on. You have got to do something.

Jesus gave this woman her son back. And the boy got up and started talking to the people who were carrying him to the grave. God is about to allow what you had that people were carrying to the grave come back to life and start talking to them.

And the bible record, the people rejoiced, they shouted that the Lord has given us a prophet and favor. And people started talking about Jesus all over the countryside, and the story was told everywhere. Maybe revival comes when people start talking about Jesus.

Don't talk about the latest gossip, talk about Jesus. Don't talk about each other, talk about Jesus. Don't talk about he say and she say, Talk about Jesus. By simply talking about the goodness of Jesus, revival jumps off on your row, in your home, in your church and in your life. Talk about Jesus and revival just might show up.

-FIVE-

Jesus raises Jairus' daughter from the dead

Mark 5:21 – 43

25 But when the people were put forth, he went in, and took her by the hand, and the maid arose.

It's Your Turn   Rev. John H. Gamble Jr.

Jesus and Jairus' Daughter

Mark 5:21 – 43

A couple went to the airport to catch their flight. When they arrived at the gate, they were told by an agent, that they had to wait to board. So they made their way to the spot in the waiting area and took a seat. They were put to the side and didn't know why.

People began boarding and as even more people boarded and time passed, the couple began getting frustrated. They were waiting and didn't know why. After a while, they started to get mad. They thought the airline was treating them poorly by making them wait with no explanation and no time frame.

Now, everyone had boarded the plane but them. They were gaping to be the last to board the plane even though they were one of the first passengers there. All kinds of things were going on in the couple's minds. They wondered what was going on. It wasn't right. They were there early.

Finally, after everyone else was on, the couple was told they could board. Frustrated, the couple walked down the jet way, and looked at their boarding passes to find their seat assignments. They didn't know, but they had been upgraded to first class! All of a sudden their sorrow became laughter. Their sadness became joy, and they added pep in their step because whereas they were scheduled for coach, they had now been moved up to first class.

They were frustrated because other people were going ahead of them. They were aggravated because they had been there first. But they learned their lesson. That sometimes when it seems like others are being blessed, and others are being moved ahead of you, it is not reason to panic, stress out, or get upset. You just have to learn to wait your turn, because oftentimes the greatest blessing comes to those who have to wait.

And this might be the lesson that Jesus is trying to teach us in the text because I would imagine that the same frustration this couple faced over their seats is the same frustration Jairus faces over his daughter. In the text, Jesus has just finished dealing with the demoniac man. You know the story. He was running through the tombs! (TELL THE STORY!)

Now Jesus gets back on the boat, crosses to the other side of the sea, and as he gets off the boat, a crowd forms around him. Jesus starts walking and a ruler of the synagogue, a man by the name of Jairus, comes to Jesus asking him to come to house and heal his daughter. You see it in the text. Verses 22, 23

> *22 And behold, one of the rulers of the synagogue came, Jairus by name. And when he saw Him, he fell at His feet 23 and begged Him earnestly, saying, "My little daughter lies at the point of death. Come and lay Your hands on her, that she may be healed, and she will live."*

Don't miss it. He is a ruler of the synagogue, but he is coming to Jesus, who is not particularly welcomed in the synagogue. As a matter of fact, one day, when he taught in the synagogue one day (Luke 4), the people became so mad that they threw him out of the city, and brought him to the edge of hill to throw him off a cliff. He was not welcomed in the synagogue. They did not want him to speak. They did not want someone in the building who would challenge their self-righteousness and their arrogance. But here is Jairus, a ruler of the synagogue who shows up to

Jesus saying, "If you come and lay hands on my daughter, I know she can be healed."

Because Jairus understood that self-righteous would not get his daughter healed. He understood that teaching the law would not get her healed…. tradition and sticking with what they always did would not get her healed. Jairus knew that she needed a touch from Jesus! He says,

> "Come and lay Your hands on her, that she may be healed, and she will live."

Perhaps Jairus was there when an unclean spirit showed up in the synagogue when the evil spirit called out Jesus as the Holy One of God, and Jesus rebuked the demon, told him to hold his peace, and then casted him out. Perhaps heard about how Jesus left the synagogue, went to the house of Peter whose mother in law was sick. He stood over her, rebuked the fever and the fever left her. He might have even been there when they lowered that paralyzed man through the roof and placed him in front of Jesus. But whatever it was that brought Jairus to Jesus, he came to Jesus expecting deliverance for his daughter.

> *I need to come expecting that the deposit I make in worship, will lead to a withdrawal of what God has in store for me.*

And I have learned that whenever I come into the presence of the Lord, I need to come expecting deliverance. I need to come expecting to leave better than I came. I need to come expecting that the deposit I make in worship, will lead to a withdrawal of what God has in store for me.

Jairus could have allowed other people's opinions to discourage him. He could have allowed what the other rulers of the synagogue might say hinder me. But Jairus decided that I can't allow what the other rulers think to prevent my daughter from getting what she needs from the Lord!

And at the end of the day, that's been my experience in my relationship with God. I've come too far to allow people's opinions of me to hinder what God is doing in me… stop the growth God is doing me in me! You may not see my growth, but I know God is working on me. I know God is improving me. I know God is making, shaping me, and molding me for his glory! (Am I by myself? Is there anybody in here who can say I've come too far to allow people to discourage me!)

So, Jairus comes to Jesus. He asks Jesus to heal his daughter. Jesus starts walking with him. It seems like Jairus is going to be blessed and his request granted. And there is an interruption. A woman with an issue of blood shows up. (We know her story) She touches the hem of Jesus garment. Her condition is dried up. Jesus was on his way to Jairus' house. But now he stops and has to deal with this woman. She is almost like a child who cuts the lunch line. Jairus had come to Jesus first. He was first on line to be blessed. But this woman gets ahead of him and gets healed.

It seems unfair. It seems like if Jesus was committed to healing Jairus' daughter than nobody else should have been able to get ahead of him. But don't miss this nuance of the text. Jairus' daughter was twelve years old. This woman had an issue of blood for 12 years! In other words, for as long as Jairus had a daughter, this woman was no able to produce. At least he could have a child. This woman could not produce. The nature of her illness, a continuous menstrual flow, made her unproductive. And

> *Sometimes God will allow them to get ahead of you on the list of his blessings because you are stronger than others who need to be blessed.*

sometimes God may not bless us immediately, because he needs to bless some people who have been unproductive, but have a desire to produce. There are some people who want to do more, but can't do more... do better, but can't seem to get over the hump. Sometimes God will allow them to get ahead of you on the list of his blessings because you are stronger than others who need to be blessed. It's like a organ transplant list. One of the leading characteristics for placing names on the list is what is called "medical urgency." In other words, the risk of that person dying may be so great that they are moved ahead of other people on the list who are stronger and have a greater chance for survival. And that's what God will do. He will move some people up the list who need to be blessed before it's too late. It doesn't mean that God has forgotten about you. It doesn't mean that God is not going to grant your request. It simply means that God is saying, "Be patient. It's not your turn."

And that's the message: What God promises may not be immediate, but it is imminent. It may not happen right now. But it will happen.

And that's what happens in the text. Jesus is walking with Jairus, stops to address this woman with an issue of blood, and now when we get to the text, verse 35 says,

35 While He was still speaking, some came from the ruler of the synagogue's house who said, "Your daughter is dead. Why trouble the Teacher any further?"

36 As soon as Jesus heard the word that was spoken, He said to the ruler of the synagogue, "Do not be afraid; only believe."

They had given up. But Jesus was not done yet. They saw the girl as dead, Jesus saw her as alive. They did not understand the Jesus they had come to. Perhaps they were used to other men who walked around claiming to heal. Perhaps they were used to other men who were wise and had good teachings. But they had never encountered Jesus who was GOD WITH US. They did not understand that when God moves, he doesn't even need to be at the house in order for healing to take place. Ask that centurion soldier who said, "Lord, I am not even worthy for you to come under my roof, just speak a word…." Jesus didn't have to even show up at the house and this little girl could have been healed!

And that's what the text is tailored to teach us. It may not happen immediately. It may not happen when we want it to happen. But it will happen!

> *It may not happen immediately. It may not happen when we want it to happen. But it will happen!*

In her book Waiting with God, Suzanna Elizabeth Anderson says, "I may never know when an answer to prayer is going to arrive, but I know that God will never fail me."

Henri Nouwen says, "We want to see results, and preferably instantly...But God works in secret and with a divine patience."

An anonymous author wrote, "Delays are not refusals… God has a set time as well as a set purpose, and He who orders the bounds of our habitation orders also the time of our deliverance."

And so, if you seek something from God, and you have not received it yet, first you need to stop listening to people and listen to God. The text says,

> *38 Then He came to the house of the ruler of the synagogue, and saw a tumult and those who wept and wailed loudly. 39 When He came in, He said to them, "Why make this commotion and weep? The child is not dead, but sleeping."*

You can't understand the significance of these verses if you have not read this text in context. Jesus is in Capernaum. He is on his way to the house. He is stopped by a woman touching him. The word comes that the girl died. And while he is walking to the house, the mourners have already shown up. If you read it in Matthew 9, it says that there were minstrels and people making noise. In other words, this girl just died, and the professional mourners have shown up along with the musicians. Now, don't miss it! A man comes from the house to tell the master that the girl died, which meant that everybody in the house knew that Jairus was leaving to find Jesus, but the minute the girl's condition goes from bad to worse, she is written off as dead. The musicians are called. The mourner are on their way. This was not like when Jesus stopped the funeral procession at the gate. This girl just died, and they are all ready to bury her, though they know help is on the way. And we have to be careful because there are people who are waiting for the indication that what ails us will ultimately kill us so they can bury us. Just because people show up by your side doesn't mean that they want you well. Look at this scene. These mourners and musician show up at the house as soon as the girl died!

And the reason why they showed up is because they stand to benefit off this girl's demise. Her death makes them money. Her death makes them useful. Think about it. How did they get to the house so fast to start playing and crying unless they started hanging around the house once they heard the little girl was sick. They were secretly waiting for her to die. And there are some people who are hanging around in your vicinity. There are some people connected to you who may see your struggles, see your issues, see your pain, and what they are waiting to do, is waiting for you to die. They are waiting for your big fall. They are waiting for you to mess up because they will profit more from you dead than alive.

Let me help you right now. Let me put it where you can get it. There are some preachers who I know can't stand me, BUT if I got sick right now, they would try to be my best friend. Watch this! Not because they care about me or they want me to be well, but they would hang around so that Smyrna would see them by my side so if or when I die, it would give them an advantage in becoming the new pastor. And there are some people who hover around your life. They check in with you not because they care, but because they stand to benefit from you.

Look at what happens in the text. They hover around the house. The girl dies and they immediately start wailing and cry. The musicians strike up the hymns. They see Jesus. They know he is there to heal the girl, but they don't change their tune.

But notice happens. They think she is dead, but Jesus said, "She is not dead, but sleeping."

And that's why you have to listen to the voice of God, and not the voices of people. Because people will write you off rather than pray you out. People will write you off in a minute. People will play you out without thinking about it. People will declare you dead without thinking about it. But Jesus is saying, "When I am in the equation, it is never as bad as it seems." And that's why we have to listen to the voice of God because God always allows us to see that there is hope in every situation. There is a silver lining in every cloud. There is a light at the end of the tunnel. And when you are in Christ, there is nothing good about you that can die, that God does not have the power to resurrect! Some of us have allowed our dreams to die... desires to die... goals and aspirations to die... getting our degree to die... buying a home, getting a promotion to die... But God says, "It is not dead, it's dormant! It's not

> *People will write you off rather than pray you out.*

time yet." But when God says it's time, He will resurrect the desires of my heart. He will give me the things I have prayed and asked God for. He will do it when it's my turn! That's why I don't allow everybody to speak over my life; I allow the word of God to speak to me! The Word says who I can be…

When it's our turn, we have to listen to the voice of God, not people. But then we have to be connected with the right people. It's in the text.

40 And they ridiculed Him. But when He had put them all outside, He took the father and the mother of the child, and those who were with Him, and entered where the child was lying. 41 Then He took the child by the hand, and said to her, "Talitha, cumi," which is translated, "Little girl, I say to you, arise."

Don't miss it. Jesus was being followed by a multitude but when he heard the girl died, he left the multitude, and even left most of the disciples. He only took with him – Peter, James, and John. He gets to the house, he encounters those mourners and musicians, who are mad that he believes the girl is dead not dormant, and he throws them out of the house. When he goes into the room, there are six people, and the girl makes seven. He brings the three disciples with the strongest faith, Jairus and his aife. H3e blocks out the people who are pessimistic and who want to focus on this girl's death and not her deliverance. He pushes them out of the house because their negative energy, will hinder, and not help what God planned to do in that place.

And sometimes in our lives, in order for God to move, it requires some realignment of the people around us. Sometimes it requires us shutting some people out. There are some relationship we need to close the door on. Not that they are bad people, but they are not on the same page as you. They want a funeral because the girl died; the parents want a celebration because she is alive. And I can't have what God has for me, if I am connected with people who are working against me. And I know we don't like it but we have to understand that we can't be connected to people who are going to pull us away from what God has for our lives. We can be cool; we just can't be connected. And let me take this a step further. Notice in the text. Jesus puts them all out. Not Jairus. Not his wife. Jesus does it! Because, as you grow in your relationship with God, God has a way of separating you, and pushing back the people who are trying to block you when it is your time to be blessed! The woman with the issue of blood was not blocking as a matter of fact, she came from behind Jesus and touched him. She didn't hinder the forward progress of Jesus. But these people were challenging if Jesus could do the very thing he came to do. And so, Jesus removes them so as not to shake the faith of these parents who came to Jesus believing that their child would live!

And as you grow in faith, God will pull you away from people who are blessing blockers. And you might be surprised who God moves out of the way. Because there are some people who will smile in your face, while they try to block your blessing. There are some people who will work against more than they will work for you. There are some people who will sing your praises, while they plan your destruction. Because there are some people who are only content in misery!

Think about it. The people who are blocking this girl from being healed are minstrels and mourners. They get paid when people are miserable. They get paid when people are mourning! Don't think that everybody who rubs your back when you cry really care. Some are rejoicing on the inside.

We need to be led by the spirit, and ask God to surround us with people who want to see us prosper who want to see us do well. I don't need a multitude of people following me. I need to be the most popular preacher. I don't need everybody to know my name. But what I need is a few people in my life who I am connected to, who will pray with me to get me through what I am going through! And you

> *Ask God to surround us with people who want to see us prosper who want to see us do well.*

may need to change your seat.... Clear out your contacts... change who follow, who you're your friends, and who you're linked in with... Because you need a strong connection!

(Talk about when they rewired the house, because the cable signal could not get to all the TVs – weak signal. I don't need to be connected to somebody with a WEAK signal!)

(Are you the one? Or should I look at someone else?)

When it's your turn, you need to stop listening to people and listen to God. You need to be connected to the right people. But finally, you need to be prepared to do your part. The Bible says,

> *41 Then He took the child by the hand, and said to her, "Talitha, cumi," which is translated, "Little girl, I say to you, arise." 42 Immediately the girl arose and walked, for she was twelve years of age. And they were overcome with great amazement. 43 But He commanded them strictly that no one should know it, and said that something should be given her to eat.*

He touched the girl. The girl got up and started walking. But then he said, "Give her something to eat." Her eating was evidence that she was not dead, but alive. If she was eating people would not fall into their superstitious thought that they were viewing a ghost. Seeing her eat was evidence that Jesus had done what he promised to do. But then, there is another benefit to her eat. She was awake. She was walking. But she was still weak. And by giving her food, it would nourish her, and prevent her from becoming sick again. Jesus is saying that once I bless you, you have to take the necessary precautions to ensure that you don't end up back in the same situation I just delivered you from. In other words, Jesus is saying, "If you don't want to be sick again, you have to prevent the illness. Give her something to eat." FEED HER.

And when God blesses us, there is evidence to convince us that it was God and God alone. And not only that, but there is also an assurance that if we nurture and nourish the blessing that he has given us, it will prevent us from having to deal with the same thing once again.

In other words, feed the girl in obedience was a sign of appreciation to Jesus, letting him know that they were going to take care of the blessing he had just giving them.

Whatever God blesses you with, you need to do whatever you can to take care of it. Because taking care of it is a sign that you are grateful.

- If he is blessed you with children, take care of them
- If he has blessed you with money, be a good steward of it!
- If he has blessed you with a house, a home, a relationship, employment: maintain it!

Because how we treat the blessings of God, shows how much we appreciate him!

It's Your Turn!

It's Revival, And Here Are The Keys   Dr. Willie J. Thompson Jr.

Matthew 8:18-26 (NLT)

18 As Jesus was saying this, the leader of a synagogue came and knelt before him. "My daughter has just died," he said, "but you can bring her back to life again if you just come and lay your hand on her." 19 So Jesus and his disciples got up and went with him. 20 Just then a woman who had suffered for twelve years with constant bleeding came up behind him. She touched the fringe of his robe, 21 for she thought, "If I can just touch his robe, I will be healed." 22 Jesus turned around, and when he saw her he said, "Daughter, be encouraged! Your faith has made you well." And the woman was healed at that moment. 23 When Jesus arrived at the official's home, he saw the noisy crowd and heard the funeral music. 24 "Get out!" he told them. "The girl isn't dead; she's only asleep." But the crowd laughed at him. 25 After the crowd was put outside, however, Jesus went in and took the girl by the hand, and she stood up! 26 The report of this miracle swept through the entire countryside.

It's Revival, and Here Are The Keys!

Do you remember the Keymaker from the film The Matrix Reloaded? Korean-American actor Randall Duk Kim, plays the fictional character called the Keymaker, a perceiving and feeling program who is not tricked by the System. Whose only job is the carve shortcut keys used by every program in the Matrix. With those keys one can move throughout the entire Matrix, being able to access any and all of its entities.

His only job was to provide shortcut keys to help people better navigate the Matrix, the virtual reality simulated world, or better yet to help people better navigate the customs, the habits, the beliefs, the values, the behavior and material habits that constitute a people's way of life. His job was to make short-cut keys, you know short keys, a shorter, quicker or easier way to get to a place. Now you could take the long route to get to a place or you can take the short-cut. The Keymaker makes shortcut keys that will take you through the behaviors of people on a more direct route and helps you to save time, energy and effort. The keymaker made short-cut keys. Now you can take six months to figure out what you brought, what you picked up and what you think you wanted is not what you got. Or you can just look at what it's doing up front and see that it's not what you want, what you got and what you need.

Now within the Matrix, the keys represent tokens of authentication used to gain access to a backdoor or to gain control of a device. And the Keymakers job was to make but not only so, but also to authenticate shortcut keys to help Neo, access the backdoor of the Architect also known as the "The Source" of the Matrix and ultimately saves the only human stronghold in the real world Zion.

I believe Matthew, the tax collector, who was accused of following Jesus with a writers pen in his hand identifies a brother who was a type of Neo, named Jarius, who would like to share with us some shortcut his shortcut keys, that allowed him to access the Architect, and in the Mathenian text he is called Jesus our King who wants us to follow and serve him. He would like to share with us the keys he used to access The Source, and in the Mathenian text he is called the Prophet, anticipated since the days and words of Moses. He would like to share with us the keys he used to access Restoration, Resurrection and Revival, and in the Mathenian text he is called our Savior, the one who helps us recover from the tragedy of our unbelief and estrangement from God.

You can take the long route to get to what you need God to bring back to you. And you can take the scenic route to your breakthrough, but maybe the record of the miracle needed by a ruler who had to go another way to get what he needed, who didn't mind going through the backdoor to the sacred place of the Architect so that he could ultimately save Zion.

Maybe the detailed Mathenian account of Jarius' miracle story will provide for us the shortcut keys to Revival.

> *Have a posture more recognizable than a position.*

I believe if Jarius was with us today he would say, the Key to access revival is to Have a posture more recognizable than a position.

We find in the opening verses that, while Jesus was speaking, a ruler of the synagogue, came up to him and knelt before him (18). Wait this was no regular man, this was a man with a position, a layman's position. He was the one who cared for the building and selected those who participated in the service. This man has an assistant and one of his main duties was to deliver the sacred scrolls to those who read and return them to the special place where they were kept. He had a position of power in the temple. And if anybody ought to get a miracle it ought to be somebody who serves in some capacity in God's house. Jarius had the right position, but the right position doesn't always get you to the architect. Because the Bible says, the man with the position ran to Jesus and knelt down and showed to us that the key is not the position, the key is in the posture.

You have to be careful when you get a position, because if that position does not allow you, when you are in trouble, to get in the right posture, you could miss your encounter. Every now and then, Ushers have to come off the doors and kneel down, every now and then, Trustees have to stop holding up the walls and bow down. Every now and then the choir ought to bow down, every now and then the preacher and the deacon ought to bow down. When was the last time, you didn't care about what people called you and thought about you and found your way to Jesus. Jarius teaches us, it's not about your position, it's about your POSTURE. And not just your poise, but your internal state and condition. It's about your attitude, it's about your frame of mind and your disposition. And if you want to access The Source and receive Revival, here is the shortcut key: have posture more recognizable than your position..

But that's not all, I believe if Jarius was with us today he would say, the second Key to access revival is to Have a problem that can only be solved through prophetic proclamation.

Verse 18 gives us some insight to this key when Jarius says, "My daughter has just died," he said, "but you can bring her back to life again if you just come and lay your hand on her."

He had a problem, but also had a proclamation over the problem he had. He had a worry, but He also had a Word from The Lord about the thing he was worried about. He saw the situation, but he also did his homework and had a statement, he could call up so that the situation could be changed. Here is the key, you must have a problem that can be solved by a prophetic proclamation..

There are some things that you can solve yourself, but if you have a problem, that is bigger than you. If you have a problem, that has superseded all of your resources and abilities. If you have a problem that you just can't solve, all you have to do is find a prophetic proclamation to speak over the problem and provide an opportunity for God to make His Word good.

Jarius says, "my daughter is dead, but you can bring her back to life again." He did his homework. I would like to suggest that because he worked in the temple and his role was to pass the scrolls to the person reading, he must have been a good churchman. By listening in on what was read every now and then. And because of what he heard he was able to access what he heard when he needed it. Sometimes, if you just keep showing up to the temple, you can overhear something, that you will be able to access in your time of need and what you heard will turn your situation all the way around. You could stay at home, but like Jarius, you might want to make your way to the temple. You have the right to do whatever you want to do on Sunday Mornings or Wednesday nights, but when you have a dead child, a dead marriage and a dead body on your hands, you might want to have heard something that you can access that will bring that dead thing back to life.

You can't access what you don't have in your possession. If you can make it to the temple, it should be a word around. And I'm not talking about gossip, I'm talking about a word that can heal the sick and raise the dead. And we have no excuse, so even if the preacher ain't preaching the word, every church has placed a bible right there in the pew, and all you got to do is pick it up and read it and you will find a word with power to change any situation.

In the scrolls, he must have heard, "he was wounded for our transgression, bruised for our iniquities, the chastisement of our peace was upon him and by his stripes we are healed.

Jarius must have heard, the power of life and death is in the tongue.

Jarius must have heard while serving in the church, yea though I walk through the valley of the shadow of death I will fear no evil, for The Lord is with me, His rod and his staff they comfort me.

You have to have something you can say, a word, that is constantly being shared at the temple, that you can access, a prophetic proclamation over your problem. "My daughter is dead, but you can bring her back to life."

But that's not all that Jarius has to share with us there is another shortcut key. If you want to access the Source and save Zion, you must: Have a need for providential privacy over pessimistic (contradictory or paradoxical) people.

In verse 23, When Jesus arrived at the official's home, he saw the noisy crowd and heard the funeral music. 24 "Get out!" he told them. "The girl isn't dead; she's only asleep."

Sometimes you have to allow God to give you some privacy by backing people out of your life, so he can help you deal with what you have to deal with. And deal with it from His providential point of view instead of peoples' pessimistic perspective.

And I'm not talking about the chaos you create, trying to push everyone away because you are afraid of people finding out who you really are. I'm talking about the privacy that comes to you as a result of God separating you to deal with you in a better way.

In the hospital system, when you have a case that requires the skill set of the intensive care unit, family and friends can only go so far with you in the process, because the doctors know that to remedy this concern, everybody can't be in the room when the doctor performs the surgery and opens you up.

Jesus shows up and hears the crowd crying and see the people talking and gathered, and they even had the nerve to laugh at Jesus and Jesus puts them all out so he can bring revival to a dead situation. And when God sees your need for privacy, you don't have to do anything, GOD

HIMSELF will put them out.

So Jarius' story comes to share with us that if you want to access the source one of the shortcut keys is, you must have a need for providential privacy over contradictory, pessimistic and paradoxical people.

Last but not least, Jarius' story as recorded by Matthew leaves with us one more shortcut Key to help us access "The Source," and provoke Revival. The last key to revival is to: Have a need for a prophet with demonstration power

The Bible says in verse, 25 After the crowd was put outside, however, Jesus went in and took the girl by the hand, and she stood up! There is a phrase, where people, when put in doubt, about something they have said, will stop using words and say, "I can show you better than I can tell you." And here Jesus enters the room, even though he was not doubted by the man with the problem, he was doubted by the poised and pessimistic people. Jesus enters the room and the story records that very simply he took the girls by the hand, and the girl stood up. It was time to talk about power, it was a time to have some power.

So many times we run to folk who can talk about our situation, but have no power to change our situation. Jarius bypasses all the others and makes his way to the prophet who has the power to change things and make everything alright.

> *So many times we run to folk who can talk about our situation, but have no power to change our situation.*

Enough talking has been going on, I believe Jesus shows up and says, I can show you better than I can tell you..

And when you get into tough situations and you have a dead thing on your hands and a prophet in your midst, you better run like Jarius, with the shortcut key so that you can access the Architect who has the power to change things.

Oh that reminds me, in the Movie the Matrix reloaded! The Oracle summons Neo, to find the Keymaker, who has the shortcut keys, so Neo can access the back door of the place where the Architect lives, who is the only one who has the power to change the situation and save Zion.

Did you know that Zion is a popular name for a little girl, and also a popular name for Gods leading lady, the people of Israel, the chosen ones of God. The old mothers back in the day, when prayers got low and praise slowed down,, would yell out "Come On Zion!"

I can hear The Oracle, the Holy Ghost, summons Neo, the Son, to go down and find the Key Maker who has the key called The Blood of the Lamb,, to give us access to The Source, God the Father, who is the only one who can Save Zion. The Church of God and The Body Of Christ. Come Zion, your Savior draws near. come on Zion, he'll wipe away all tears, Come Zion, he will take away all Fears. Come Zion, if you lift Him High, Come On Zion, Your joy you will find.

You can take the long route, or you can take the shortcut key and cause Revival to Break out in your Life. It's Revival...

-SIX-

Matthew 21:4-5 (MSG)

4-5 This is the full story of what was sketched earlier by the prophet:
Tell Zion's daughter, "Look, your king's on his way, poised and ready,
mounted on a donkey, on a colt, foal of a pack animal."

He Had To Come This Way   Dr. Willie J. Thompson Jr.

Matthew 21:4-5 (MSG)

4-5 This is the full story of what was sketched earlier by the prophet: Tell Zion's daughter, "Look, your king's on his way, poised and ready, mounted on a donkey, on a colt, foal of a pack animal."

Its Revival: He Had to Come This Way

Isaiah chapters 56-66 are found in a section called 3rd Isaiah. The audience is once more living in the land of Judah. They have returned from Babylonian exile. And this is the second time they have been brought back from captivity. The problem is that this return, this second deliverance is not as glorious as it was predicted to be. For life for the returnees in Judah remains very harsh. There is economic oppression and to deal or cope with harsh conditions and economic oppression the people are returning to pagan rituals that they once favored in Israel. In response to this, God through Isaiah announces God's imminent judgment on the oppressors and syncretists and that deliverance is on the way.

But before you shout about the deliverance let's explore the context of Israel's condition. They have just got out of a repeat of history. They have found themselves delivered from some of the same oppressive situations as their forefathers experienced. Delivered twice. Strayed, caught, heard and delivered. Strayed again, caught again, heard again and delivered again. Wandered off, again. Got caught up, again. Cried for help, again, and brought back again. But for Israel the return to the land of their home was different than what had previously happened and especially different from what was expected.

Have you ever gotten in trouble twice and found out that the mercy you got the second time, was slightly different than the mercy or slap on the hand you got the first time?

Israel has once again been retrieved from the tyrannical oppressive structures of a ruthless oppressor, by an almighty and everlasting God. But this time the return home is not the cake walk that it was the first time. For the people of God did not just return home to a Welcome Home Party, but they also had to deal with harsh living conditions and economic oppression and a struggle that they did not consider on the other side of their breakthrough in Judah.

You know how it is in Judah. Judah was a city founded or established by a people who had a history of dealing with dirty money, and a stronger history of dirty transactions. You know Judah had three sons, and two of them were slain by the Lord because of their wickedness and contempt of God. You know that son Onan, who was disobedient to God and disrespected God by spilling his seed instead of reproducing. There it is, a history of dirty transactions. Judah's son, Onan, who has something in him that could produce and refused to put it where it belonged so that it could bring for life. Judah, you know Judah who had twin sons, Pharez and Zarah. And that one son Pharez was not the first to come out, but was willing to do what it took to always be on top. He even, when his brother was coming out of the womb before him, grabbed his brother's foot and pulled him back down into the womb so that he could come out first. You know that's dirty. Israel have just come out of their second slavery and now they are in a land that is characterized by dirty transactions. Surrounded by dirty dealings and more problems.

You know what's going on in Judah, don't you remember that Judah was the brother of Joseph, that said, when they were going to kill their brother

125

for being a dreamer. "Brothers, let's not kill him, let's just sell him to the Ishmaleites (Gen. 37:25-27)." The people are surrounded by dirty dealing and dirty transactions. Judah was home, but Judah had problems. They had economic problems, they didn't want to pay their bills. And they wanted to spend money they didn't have. Babylon had taken ten thousand captive, taken all of their men of valor, and all of their craftsmens and smiths and left only the poorest people in town.

Have you ever gotten out of Big trouble, only to come home and find more trouble?

What about money trouble, opportunity trouble, people trouble, job trouble, school trouble, community trouble, marriage trouble, health trouble. It seems like you can't win for losing. Child trouble, mind trouble, can't stay away from trouble. Israel was free and delivered but in trouble.

And people when they are in trouble, even when they have been brought out of a bad situation by God, will sometimes turn to anything to find relief. And find a way to cope with the problem they are facing in life.

And I know because of our Israelite-ness we will always do what is right, but I want you to consider this bunch of Israelites and God's chosen people, who did not run to the church or the temple when life had weighed them down, they ran back to what they used to do. Not because they are evil. Not because they are non-believers, but when situations get hard people try to find ways to cope. And how you did it always looks easier than what you cannot not see in your future.

I know you don't but, 52% or released prisoners, those who have served their time, paid their debt, end up right back in prison, because when they get out they can't find jobs, they are disowned by their families and they are not trusted, and when it gets hard like this, they end up going right back to what they knew. (Crime In America.net)

I know you don't but 1 in 4 people who complete a drug rehabilitation program or intervention will return back to drugs within 3 months of completion, because when life gets hard people sometimes go back to what they knew .

I know you don't do this but. 73% of lung cancer survivors still smoke. Women who are in domestically abusive relationships sometimes leave, get out in the world and find no help, sometimes go back. And to be clear, of the 71% of people who start dieting, go right back to their eating habits right after they attend the event they started dieting for. Sometimes when life gets hard people get worse.

> *Of the 71% of people who start dieting, go right back to their eating habits right after they attend the event they started dieting for.*

And in our text it is apparent that the harsh living conditions were taking a toll on the people. In this text it is apparent that the economic oppression was taking a toll on the people and to cope with life they began to tap into pagan and idolatrous worship that led them further away from God. Strayed, strayed again, captured, captured again, heard, heard again, delivered and delivered again and now worse than we were before.

Surrounded by dirty dealings, and feelings of hopelessness have set in. And feelings of abandonment have set in. And feelings of being played have set in. And now we don't even look like or reflect the God we have been called to serve.

And the prophet Isaiah, rises up and says to these people, "Look, listen, God's arm is not amputated—he can still save! God's ears are not stopped up—He can still hear. There's nothing wrong with God; the wrong is in you.

Israel there are some sins and iniquities that have separated you from God and distanced God's ability to hear your concerns and answer. In Israel there is an overwhelming current of guilt, lies, obscenities, silence. You talk when you should not and you are silent when you should talk. Israel there are some unfair deals, lies, mischief, wickedness, violence, evil doings, murder, mistreatment, peace breaking and case stacking going on and are acting like you don't see it.

You do remember Tyler Perry's movie "Madea Goes To Jail?" The movie picks up where Meet the Browns ends, with Madea and Uncle Joe, both played by Tyler Perry, are involved in a high car speed chase with the police. However because of a technicality (the office forgets to read Medea her Miranda rights) the judge Mablean Ephriam is forced to let her go. Later on Madea destroys a lady's car and is sent to jail again by Judge Greg Mathis and is sent to jail. Madea is one of seven young ladies who ends up with TRUMPED up charges and are wrongly convicted the charges eventually get overturned. But that's not always the case. But in Judah, Israel knew of some people with trumped up charges and did nothing.

Israel there is some inhumane treatment, falsity, stumbling, darkness, groaning, moaning and a seeking after justice and salvation, but none readily available.

But Israel is not in the dark about their wrong doings. The text makes it clear that what they are doing wrong is actually staring back at them. It's not a mystery or a case to be solved. Israel you mock and deny God;

spread rumors, incite sedition, mutter malice, beat back justice, push righteousness to the side; you give no place for truth, (truth is drunk in love); you have the inability to be honest, can't find any good anywhere. And Israel you beat and rob anyone who renounces evil, surrounded by dirty dealings and shaky transactions. Wasting what God has placed down inside of you. Throwing rocks and hiding your hand. Giving in to the organized plans of the enemy. Taking each other out. Selling each other off, pulling each other back down, just so you can come out on top. And you would think that being surrounded by evil was enough but the bible says:

"God looked and saw evil looming on the horizon." (MSG v.15)

So God had to Come this way because: God is paying attention to what is ahead of us and not just what is in front of us.

> *God is paying attention to what is ahead of us and not just what is in front of us.*

He had to come this way not only because of what we were dealing with right in front of us, but He saw what was coming down the road. While we sometimes just think that the here and now is all that there is, God has the ability to see what we can not see. Don't that remind you of that famous Jeremiah text, reminding people who are in trouble, to hold on because *"I know the thoughts and the plans I have towards you, the plans of good and not evil designed to bring you out to an expected end."* (Jer. 29:11).

God says, I know your end from the beginning. I am the Alpha and the Omega. I had to come this way to see what you can not see and to protect you from what you cannot see and to show you what you cannot see.

God knew what was ahead of them and not just in front of them. And not only so, but also he knew what he was going to do about what you were facing. In 2nd Chronicles 20:15, The Lord said, ``Listen King Jehoshaphat and all who live in Judah and Jerusalem, "Do not be afraid of this vast army that stands before you, for the battle is not yours, it belongs to the Lord."

He had to come because He's paying attention to what's ahead of us and not just what's in front of us. The Bibles goes on to say in the challenging situation:

"He couldn't believe what He saw: not a soul around to correct the situation." (MSG v.16)

So God had to come this way because: God was amazed that the people who should be concerned, were not concerned at all.

And the amplified version says, "no man" and wondered that there was "no intercessor," (AMP) no one to intervene on the behalf of truth and right." No one to correct this awful situation. God was amazed, and possibly could not understand, how people who have a rich history of oppression, completely forget where they came from and have the nerve to participate in the oppression of others. If anybody out to be fighting for justice and equality, it should be people who have been treated unjustly and as unequal.

Exodus 1:8, says "Now there arose up another king who didn't know Joseph. He said to his people in alarm. There are way too many of them. We have got to do something about them. Put them in work gangs, and let us PROFIT off of them." Shady, and dirty transactions.

If anybody out to be fighting for justice and equality, it should be people who have been treated unjustly and as unequal.

In the 72 years between the election of George Washington and Abraham Lincoln, there arose a king who knew not Joseph, and said Let us deal with them. Let us put them in work gangs and let us profit off of them.

If anybody out to be fighting for justice and equality, it should be people who have been treated unjustly and as unequal.

And now we fight over Jordans, We celebrate mediocrity. We refuse to graduate middle school let alone high school or college. We take for granted the blood and sweat and tears of our ancestors. And I'm not talking about mamma nem, I'm talking about the people who made us go to church. And made us sit in Bible study and made us serve our God and help each other. And now we don't even know how to treat ourselves equally and with justice. If anybody out to be fighting for justice and equality, it should be people who have been treated unjustly and as unequal.

You know what it feels like, but the Bible says that God was displeased and amazed that there was no man, and no intercessor to speak on the behalf of the truth and righteousness.

He was displeased because he saw intercessors and intervenors take off the task of intercession and become intoxicated in a state of individualistic interrogation. They stopped standing in the gap for others and started only praying for themselves. So God had to come this way. They forgot the scripture that said, Pray for one another, and the effectual fervent prayers of the righteous availeth much.

But not only those two reasons, but lastly. God looked and saw evil looming on the horizon, he saw something bad coming. God was displeased because there were no intercessors to correct, but here we find God entering into a conversation with Gods self. And the Bible says:

"So he did it himself, took on the work of Salvation, fueled by his own righteousness." (MSG v. 16)

God had to come this way because: "God knew that the people had more than an external societal problem, but they had an internal sin problem that only God could fix."

He said, I'm gonna have to get some help to my people. I planted some prophets, but that didn't work. I planted some storms, but that didn't work. I sent a few oppressors to redirect them, thinking that would work. I cried aloud and spare not, and that didn't work. I sent some intercessors, but that didn't work.

But then God remembered that they didn't have a hearing problem. They didn't have a memory problem. They did not have a drug or addiction problem. They did not have a personality disorder or a people problem. They, his people, only had one problem. If this problem would get fixed, all others will be solved. The problem was right there all along, but have not been dealt with, These God fearing folk had a Sin Problem. And the only way sin could be dealt with is through the blood of an unblemished sacrifice.

So he did it himself. He took on the work of Salvation!

He dressed himself in righteousness. Put salvation on His head like a helmet. He put on an overcoat called judgment. He put on a cloak of passion on his shoulders. He needed to be fully dressed for what he had to do. Because the case was serious and his people were in danger. I can hear the people saying, Ride on King Jesus, no man cannot hinder thee.

How do I know it, because in the text, the enemy was coming in like a flood, and whenever the enemy comes in like a flood the Spirit of the Lord will lift a standard against him. He had to come this way, because the people didn't have a social problem, they had a sin problem. And Tide can't wash it out. Turpentine can't spot it out. Club Soda can't blot it out. Cold water can't dilute it out. It takes blood to deal with Sin.

This is the kicker right here. Verse 20 says I'll arrive in Zion as Redeemer to those in Jacob who leave their sin. Zion… Hmmmm. Hold that point Zion…

He told Daniel and Gabriel to stand down. He told cherubim and the seraphim to hold back. He told the 24 elders to hold on praising him for just a second. He looked out among his company and said I will do this one myself.

FAST FORWARD (BLUP BLUP BLUP)

He came down forty and two generations. He wrapped himself in flesh. Implanted himself in a womb of a virgin. Was born in a meek and lowly stable. Was found in the temple at 12. Taught people how to pray. Called not the righteous, but sinners unto repentance. Declared Himself as Lord of the Sabbath. Taught on the Kingdom of God. Walked on water. Fed 5000 with seven loaves and a few fish. Healed Jarius' daughter. Talked about faith the size of a mustard seed. But he still saw the same problem. It was not society, it was the sin and it takes blood to deal with sin.

So here is Jesus. Dressed in righteousness. Had on a helmet of salvation. Had on the overcoat of judgment and a cloak of passion on his shoulders. And that passion said to his disciples; Go over to the village, and you will find a donkey, tied with her colt. Lose them and if anybody asks you, tell them, the Master has a need for them.

> *He had to come because he knew what was ahead and not just what was insight.*

And here is the good spot. Isaiah started something that Matthew had to finish. Verse 4-5 in the Message Translations, says "Tell Zion's Daughter. Look at you kings on his way. Poised, ready and mounted." He had to come because he knew what was ahead and not just what was insight. He had to come this way, because he saw that there was no man that could handle it. He had to come this way, because society was not the problem but sin was the problem. And he had to come. Because He had to keep his word, not only with the generations of the past, those of the present and the future.

And when he got there, they cried out Hosanna, Blessed is the One who comes in the name of the Lord.

But he did not stop there, because there was a SIN problem that only he could fix. He looked at the work order and the solution said BLOOD.

So he kept on going until they found him in a Garden called Gethsemane. He kept on going until he stood before an unjust council. He kept on going until he was treated like something he was not. He kept on going until they whipped it out of him. He kept on going until they nailed it out of him. He kept on going until it flowed down the old rugged cross. He kept on going until the blood hit the streets of Jerusalem, and the dead began to get up and walk.

He kept on going until he solved the real problem. He died right there to solve the real problem. He kept on going until the sun refused to shine. He kept on going until the moon dripped away in blood. He kept on going until Hell caught on fire and not flames of fire but caught Holy Ghost fire. He kept on going until he snatched the keys of hell death and the grave. You can't get in unless he sends you. And you can't get out unless he opens the door for you. He kept on going until early Sunday morning, when he got up with all power in his hand.

And Zion, if you accept his offer. And if you accept his payment for your stuff. One day, when he returns. He will say to you, come ye blessed of my father, and inherit the place prepared for you.

He had to come this way.

-SIX-

Jesus raises Lazarus from the dead

John 11:43-44 (KJV)

43 And when he thus had spoken, he cried with a loud voice, Lazarus, come forth.

44 And he that was dead came forth, bound hand and foot with graveclothes: and his face was bound about with a napkin. Jesus saith unto them, Loose him, and let him go.

GOD DID IT!   Rev. John H. Gamble Jr.

JESUS AND LAZARUS

JOHN 11

Dr. Tony Evans gives a fascinating illustration to explain our requests and God's response. He says,

> SOME people use "pop-up" timers when they cook their turkeys. This apparatus is designed to be stuck way down in the turkey and as the turkey heats up, the rising temperature registers with the thermometer. When the turkey gets fully cooked, the outside of the thermometer pops up and the turkey is done.

> But now, this only works if it is stuck way down into the inner core of the turkey because if the turkey is not cooked, then it is not ready to eat. When the inner core is right, the external thing pops out signaling that it's time to eat!

> Many people are waiting for God to pop up and say that He will give them the desires of their heart. But what they don't realize is that God is waiting for them to be fully cooked. He's waiting on them to be "done" and they just haven't finished cooking yet.

> In other words, sometimes we are waiting God to respond, and God is waiting for us to be ready.

God wants us to understand that He does not bless us because he has to. He blesses us because He chooses to bless us.

And let me suggest that this is the lesson that is tapered on this text because in this text, we are reading what is, perhaps, the most popularly preached miracle in scripture. There are not many people who have been in church, who have not heard at least one sermon about Lazarus. It has been preached and re-preached. We know the story. Jesus gets to Bethany. The reality of Lazarus' death sets in. Jesus cries, and then wants to see where Lazarus is laid. Jesus speaks to the people and says, "Who is going to roll away the stone?" Martha is concerned because Lazarus has been dead four days and the body is decomposing. It is certain to be a smell in the sepulcher. But Jesus enters into the tomb and cries out, "Lazarus, come forth!" Lazarus starts walking, bound in his grave clothes. Jesus declares, "Loose him, and let him go." It's good preaching text! As a matter of fact, I don't know a pastor who hasn't preached this text! Because here is a man dead four days! And Jesus shows up and brings him back to life! And that's exciting. It's good preaching! It's good encouragement! And it is good to know that it's never too late for God to do the miraculous in your life. It's never too late for God to turn your situation around. It's never too late for God to work things out for your good!

(And that ought to help somebody today who feels like they are at the end of their rope…. They are ready to quit, and throw in the towel… who has been counted out… and who has already been down on the scorecard of your life. God can turn every situation around!)

> *What separates this resurrection from any of the other resurrections is that this was the only time when God, or any representative of God, heard somebody was sick and they intentionally waited for them to die.*

That should be the encouragement of this text! But let me suggest that there is a deeper understanding that God is trying to get us to see in this text that may not shout us, but will no doubt change us! What separates this resurrection from any of the other resurrections is that this was the only time when God, or any representative of God, heard somebody was sick and they intentionally waited for them to die. It's right in the text.

> *1 Now a certain man was sick, Lazarus of Bethany, the town of Mary and her sister Martha. 2 It was that Mary who anointed the Lord with fragrant oil and wiped His feet with her hair, whose brother Lazarus was sick. 3 Therefore the sisters sent to Him, saying, "Lord, behold, he whom You love is sick." 4 When Jesus heard that, He said, "This sickness is not unto death, but for the glory of God, that the Son of God may be glorified through it." 5 Now Jesus loved Martha and her sister and Lazarus. 6 So, when He heard that he was sick, He stayed two more days in the place where He was.*

Lazarus is sick! Jesus doesn't move. Is that what happened in the past? Whenever there has been an issue Jesus has immediately started toward the house!

- The centurion soldier, whose servant was sick… He sends word to Jesus, saying, "Lord, I am not worthy that thou should come under my roof: but just speak the word only, and my servant shall be healed." Jesus speaks, the servant recovered.

- Jairus' daughter is sick to the point of death. Jesus gets up, starts walking toward the house. She dies on the way. Jesus doesn't stop. He keeps going until he gets there.

Wherever there is an issue, Jesus showed up. However, this time, with the people whom He was closest to, Mary and Martha, when he gets the word that Lazarus is sick, he doesn't get up and go. He stays where he is. Not just for a few hours. He stays for two more days!

Don't miss it! Jerusalem is two miles from Bethany. A leisure walking pace is 3.5 miles per hour. Jesus could have been there in less than an hour, healed Lazarus preventing his death, and then been on to do something else, but instead, Jesus waited for Lazarus to die!

Here is a man whom He loved. Here are two sisters he called friends, but when they needed him the most, it seemed like He was not there! Jesus could have made it there before he died, if he could have spoken the word and healed him before he died, and he would not have died. But the text is showing us that God's distance does not imply his disinterest!

It's in the text. He hears Lazarus is sick. He replies "This sickness is not unto death, but for the glory of God, that the Son of God may be glorified through it.", and He stayed two more days in the place where He was. Where was he? John 10 would suggest that he was in the temple, teaching and preaching. And as a result, many people were coming to believe on him.

Don't miss it! Mary and Martha already believed. Jesus was ministering to those who didn't believe that they might believe. If Jesus would have left these people who did not believe to go to Mary and Martha who did believe, he would have been leaving those who really needed him.

And perhaps, sometimes God does not respond immediately to your requests, because the sense of urgency is somewhere. Simply put: There could be someone else who needs God more than you. Just because God is present everywhere and He knows all things does not mean that He is available to answer every request at our command. We have to be careful not to treat God like a genie in a lamp, where he comes out to grant our wishes. We are created to serve Him. Not the other way around. And the reality is that whatever God does for us is not to make us feel good. God doesn't do anything for us because we command it of Him. Whatever

God does ultimately will bring him glory! And we have to stop thinking that God is absent from us when He is not doing for us.

We have to learn to let God be God, and understand the things we cannot control. Sometimes life is like flying on an airplane. One thing that makes me nervous is when I am scheduled to land, but I can't land. I can look out the window, see the airport, see the runway, and even see the city I am headed to, but we are in the air, in a holding pattern, because traffic control will not give us clearance to land. And I don't like it because I am in the air. I don't have control. I am wondering about whether the plane has enough fuel to land. But then I have to remind myself of when there is air traffic control in the first place. I am looking out my window and I can see the runway. But Air traffic controller not only sees the runway, but air traffic control can see where other planes are relative to my plane. They know the safety status of all the planes in the air. They can see things that I can't see, and just because I can't land doesn't mean there is not somebody in control.

> *God is like air traffic control. God can see what I can't see. He has a better view of the circumstances than I have.*

And God is like air traffic control. God can see what I can't see. He has a better view of the circumstances than I have. And if he chooses to land another plane before my plane, if we chooses to bless someone else before he blesses me, it doesn't mean that he was not interested; it just means that it wasn't my time! But my time is coming!

And those of us who claim to know God.... Love God... have to take God off of our timetable, and trust God and believe that he can handle it, because He knows all about it. That classic gospel song says,

You can't hurry my God. No. No. You just have to wait. You have to trust Him and give Him time. No matter how long it takes. He'll be there in a hurry. He'll be there. Don't you worry! He may not come when you want him, but He's always on time!

He wants them to understand that His distance does not mean His disinterest.

But then he takes this a step further, because I believe the text is showing us that Jesus needed to stretch Mary and Martha's faith. They needed to see Jesus as more than a faithful friend; they needed to see Him as their sovereign Savior.

In other words, they had a relationship with Jesus (as their friend), but they did not know him (as their savior). And so Jesus allows Lazarus to die, then raises Lazarus from death into new life to show Mary and Martha, as well as you and I, that we serve a God who is more than just a friend, but who, in fact, saves us because he loved us and had the sovereign power to do so.

The famous Christian author Max Lucado, in his book A Gentle Thunder says, "There are many reasons God saves you: to bring glory to himself, to appease his justice, to demonstrate his sovereignty. But one of the sweetest reasons God saved you is because he is fond of you."

And while Max Lucado is brilliant with his words, and certainly John saves us because loved us, love was not enough! And we have to understand that salvation is as much about God's love as it is about God's sovereign power.

Let me put this where we can get it. If one of my sons were to commit a crime, my love is now played against my sovereignty. I may love them. Of course, I would want them to go free. I would want them punished by my standards. BUT because I have no sovereignty over the legal system,

I cannot determine the timetable for when the trial would take place, who's on the jury, the outcome of the trial. I have my love, but there are other pieces that are out of my control. That's the difference between us and God! God loves us but He also has sovereignty. God's sovereignty is God's ability to do whatever God wants to do whenever God wants to do it. While Mary/Martha know Jesus loves them, they know Jesus has power to heal, they have to understand that he functions not just in love, but in sovereignty. God works on his timetable and in His will.

And because they are focused on the love of their friendship and not the sovereignty of his Lordship, Mary and Martha cannot see that Christ, being God, was sovereign over everything, even in death. That's what Jesus is teaching her in the text!

Jesus heard Lazarus was sick. He stayed two days where he was. Once he heard Lazarus died then he began his journey to Bethany. By the time he got there, the Bible says, that "he found that Lazarus had been the grave for four days already. Mary and Martha are in mourning. There are surrounded by those who have come from Jerusalem and the surrounding villages, to mourn the death of her brother. Martha hears that Jesus is on his way. Martha decides she can't wait until he gets there. She runs out of the house and meets Jesus on the road. Martha says,

Lord, if thou hadst been here, my brother had not died. (v21)

The problem with Martha is this: Martha could not see that God is still sovereign in suffering. She felt that Jesus could have prevented it all.

Lord, if thou hadst been here, my brother had not died. (v21)

After all, He was Jesus, and Jesus was always fixing things. She believes that Jesus could make everything alright. So Martha's upset. She feels that this shouldn't have happened, because where Jesus shows up, people are healed.... delivered... set free. But, Martha didn't understand that the death of Lazarus was in the divine plan. Whether Jesus was in Bethany or not, Lazarus was going to get sick and Lazarus was going to die. But, in his sickness, in his death, God had a greater purpose in mind.

When they first came to Jesus and told him Lazarus was sick, Jesus said,

> *This sickness is not unto death, but for the glory of God, that the Son of God might be glorified thereby. (v4)*

And Jesus didn't move. Jesus didn't move because he already knew what was going to happen. Yes, he knew the mourners would come... they would bury him... they would lament and be troubled... but Jesus knew that when it was all over, when he showed up, that He would be glorified. They would know that He was Lord, and if you keep reading the text, you will see that because of what Jesus did with Lazarus, the bible says that many who witnessed it believed!

We have to understand that with trouble comes trust. With conflict comes confidence. With adversity comes assurance. With misfortune comes faith.

> *With trouble comes trust. With conflict comes confidence. With adversity comes assurance. With misfortune comes faith.*

We make the mistake of thinking that when we call on God, he is just supposed to show up and save us from whatever situation we're in. Trouble is just supposed to disappear when God is present. We are so much like Martha. Somewhere in our lives, all of us have had a "Lord, if you would have been here" moment. When problems occur, we ask, "Where is God?"

- ▪ When someone dies

- When war breaks out

- Tragedies like school shootings, or what happened on the military base in Fort Hood,

Whenever life seems to move out of balance, we ask, "Where is God?" because we think where God is, there is no confusion as if God somehow relinquishes his ability to be all-present and all-powerful because we are having a difficult time.

We talk Bible about how God is not the author of confusion and how where the Spirit of the Lord is, there is liberty. But I need to help you out and let you know that that nowhere in scripture does it promise that there will not be troubling times, but what scripture tells us that regardless of the circumstance, God already sees. He already knows... and he already has a plan! God's plan does not preclude our suffering.

- That's why Isaiah says, "No weapon that is formed against me...." (It will formed)
- That's why David proclaims, "Yea, though I walk through...." (There will be some dark days)

As a matter of fact, God uses every situation, good and bad, to reveal himself and to bring him glory!

Remember earlier I talked about when I fly I don't like to be in a holding pattern where I can't land, and I have to trust air traffic control to see what I can't see, but what's worse than a holding pattern when I'm flying is turbulence. Turbulence is when the plane hits particular pockets of air that seem to create bumps in what should otherwise be a smooth ride. Like most people, at 37000 feet in the air, it's nerve racking for the plane to be moving like that. And in order to get out of the turbulence, you have to trust the pilot to either fly over it or navigate through it. But see, here is the difference between us and the pilot. We view turbulence as a matter of safety; the pilot looks at it as a matter of convenience. In other words, for the pilot, he is just as confident that he is going to get you where you need to go, regardless of the turbulence because he is going to get you to fly above it, or fly through.

And that's what happens when we trust a sovereign. God will lead us to a place where we can fly through it, or fly above it!

You see, Martha/Mary said, Lord, if you would have been here, my brother would not have died. But when you understand who Jesus is, you will not say, "Lord, if...," you can actually say, "Lord, now that you are here, my brother can live again!

Because, if I understand the sovereignty of God, it doesn't matter how bad the situation is... how dark the night is... how much death comes..., I know that God is in control, and He get help me get through it! Or get over it!

Sovereignty says that nothing can stop God from being God. You don't believe me. Verse 15, Jesus says to his disciples,

> Lazarus is dead. And I am glad for your sakes that I was not there, to the intent ye may believe; nevertheless let us go unto him.

16 Then Thomas, who is called the Twin, said to his fellow disciples, "Let us also go, that we may die with Him."

Thomas says what the rest of the disciples are probably thinking. The disciples were afraid they were going to die. The plan was to stone Jesus and anyone with him if he returned to Bethany. But, Jesus goes anyway. He travels back through the place he was hated the most to reach those whom He loved the most. Notice in the text, even though there are plans to take Jesus out. There are plots to kill him. He goes untouched! He goes to Lazarus! He raises Lazarus! And people believe! Because He is sovereign, nothing can stop God from being GOD!

That's why no matter how much people try to discredit faith… talk about there is no God… question the Bible, whenever trouble comes, churches are filled. Countries are praying. Preachers are called to the forefront.

Because nothing can stop God from being God!

Distance does not imply disinterest. God is sovereign, even in suffering, but then the text shows us that God's authority is absolute. Verse 22 – 25, Martha says,

> Lord, if thou hadst been here, my brother had not died. But I know, that even now, whatsoever thou wilt ask of God, God will give it thee.

Jesus says, Thy brother shall rise again.

Martha said unto Jesus, "I know that he shall rise again in the resurrection at the last day."

Jesus said unto her, I am the resurrection, and the life: he that believes in me, though he was dead, yet shall he live: And whosoever lives and believes in me shall never die. Do you believe this?

Let's stop right there. Again, it seems as though Martha is saying the right thing. She says, "I know that whatever you ask of God, he will give it to you." Jesus tells her that her brother will live and she says, "I know he will rise, when everyone else rises, in that last day." Martha does not understand that Jesus is God, she only sees him as one who has access to God. So, she begins to speak of end times. She only believes that Lazarus can rise at the time of last day resurrection. She limits the ability of God to a specific point in the future, rather than understanding the power of God to change immediately.

God's sovereignty affords God absolute authority. He can make immediate changes. But, because she wasn't connecting Jesus' divinity and humanity, she could not see that He was able to bring Lazarus to life now. So, Jesus has to get her to see the connection. Jesus says, "I am the resurrection and the life." When Jesus says, "I am", he is not referring to a future expectation; He is speaking to the present situation. Jesus is not speaking about the last day; He is speaking about TODAY. "I am" present tense, meaning, I can give Lazarus life now. Jesus is saying, "I can change the situation immediately, right now, in the present." I operate in the confines of my own schedule. In other words, Jesus is saying, "my authority is absolute." If Lazarus can get up in the last days, he can get up now!"

It's important to understand that even when it seems like God is not moving, Jesus can change a situation immediately. If Jesus knows about, He has the power to change my situation immediately and without question. In other words, when Jesus raises Lazarus, there will be no doubt that it was the Lord!

You see, by Jesus waiting until Lazarus was absolutely dead, there could be no mistake about who raised him up. You see, in the Jewish culture, there were intriguing beliefs about death. The Jews believed that the spirit of the recently dead would hover over the waiting and looking for a way to re-enter the body. If the soul could not re-enter the body, the soul would then leave the body to itself. Often the people would go to the tomb for three days, believing the soul was still there. But the fourth day would be the day of great lament because at that point, they believed that there would be no possibility of the person being resurrected. So Jesus waits until the fourth day, when the circumstance seems impossible to show up in Bethany, because Jesus doesn't want any doubts. He wants to know that it was Him who raised Lazarus up. He's sovereign in suffering, His authority is absolute, and His work is without question. What Jesus was going to do for Lazarus only He could do and when you have faith in God, and God brings life into your dead situation, you will not question that it was God.

So the Bible says, Jesus said to them, Take away the stone. Martha said, "Lord, by this time he stinks: for he has been dead four days." In other words, she had no doubt that he was dead. And she didn't know for sure that Jesus could raise him up. So, she was, in fact, saying, Jesus, just let him rest. Leave him alone. But, Jesus said,

> Did I not say to you that if you had faith you would see the glory of God?

Then they took away the stone from the place where Lazarus laid. And Jesus lifted up his eyes, gave thanks to the Father, and cried with a loud voice, Lazarus, come forth.

And the Bible says,

> And he who was dead came out… Then a number of the Jews who had come to Mary and had seen the things which Jesus did had belief in him

And sometimes, God has to allow you to deal with the most difficult of circumstances so when he brings you out, you are clear that it was God who brought you out!

Let me close with this very popular story.

The story is told of a wonderful, elderly, Christian lady. She had very little money and lived in a rundown house, but she was always praising the Lord. Her only problem was with the old man who lived next door. He was always trying to prove to her that there was no God. One day, as the old man was walking by her house, he noticed the woman through an open window. She was kneeling down in prayer, so he crept over to the window to see if he could hear. She was praying, "Lord, you've always given me what I've needed." She prayed. "And now you know that I don't have any money, and I'm completely out of groceries, and I won't get another check for a week." She continued, "Somehow, Lord, can you get me some groceries." The man had heard all he needed. He crept away from the window and ran down to the grocery store. He bought milk, bread, and lunchmeat. He ran back to the woman's house carrying the groceries. He set the bag down on by her door, rang the doorbell, and hid beside of the house. You can imagine how the woman reacted to seeing the bag of groceries. She threw her hands over head and began praising the Lord. "Thank you Jesus," she shouted. "I was without food and you provided the groceries." About that time the old man jumped out and said, "I've got you now." She was too busy shouting thank you to Jesus to pay any attention. "I told you there was no God," the old man said, "it wasn't Jesus who gave you those groceries it was me." "Oh no," the woman said. "Jesus got me these groceries and made the devil pay for them."

It's Revival, But You Got To Believe   Dr. Willie J. Thompson Jr.

John 11:38-44 (NRSV)

38 Then Jesus, again greatly disturbed, came to the tomb. It was a cave, and a stone was lying against it. 39 Jesus said, "Take away the stone." Martha, the sister of the dead man, said to him, "Lord, there is already a stench because he has been dead for four days." 40 Jesus said to her, "Did I not tell you that if you believed, you would see the glory of God?" 41 So they took away the stone. And Jesus looked upward and said, "Father, I thank you for having heard me. 42 I knew that you always hear me, but I have said this for the sake of the crowd standing here, so that they may believe that you sent me." 43 When he had said this, he cried with a loud voice, "Lazarus, come out!" 44 The dead man came out, his hands and feet bound with strips of cloth, and his face wrapped in a cloth. Jesus said to them, "Unbind him, and let him go."

You Got To Believe!

Do you know the power of belief? Do you know how strong, courageous and confident a person is who believes: A person who has a conviction that a person or thing is, has been, or will be engaged in a given action or involved in a certain situation. Have you ever met a believer: a person who has confidence in a truth; A person who relies on something and does so without absolute proof that they are right in doing so. Do you know the power of belief?

Do you know the power of belief?

Believing will cause you to lean on, trust in and walk into some things

151

that others will clearly run away from. Just ask Ashford and Simpson. Nick Ashford was inspired by an experience when he first moved to New York, while walking down a Manhattan thoroughfare, determined that New York City would not get the best of him; and the words "Ain't no Mountain high enough" popped into his head.

Believing, accepting and embracing something as the truth, a fact and a conviction will cause you to hang on to somebody after they are gone and moved on with their lives and you are still holding on to what you believed you all could have had and everybody else is tired of hearing about it. Just ask Smokey Robinson, who was so convicted that he said, "I don't care if they start to avoid me, I don't care what they do, I don't care about anything else, but being with you, being with you."

Have you ever met somebody that believes in something, they are persuaded, they have faith in it and they act like it and they live in accordance with what they believe. Almost like a fanatic, devoted to a concept, a thought or a person. A mother or father who believes in their child so they show up to games, near or far, come hell or highwater. They are always there simply because they believe. A brother or sister, that believes that something is coming for them, it's just around the corner, and every time you see them they are looking in earnest expectation for what is coming their way. And they have no reason, no evidence that it is coming, but they believe. These people have no job right now but got a resume prepared. These people have no mates right now, but they got their business fixed ready to get married. These people are not rich right now, but they are doing wisely with what they already have. These people may not have the victory right now, but when you see them, they look like they got it. These people have pains running all through their bodies, but they make their way to the House of God and lift up holy hands like everything is alright. They have no evidence, no absolute proof, no confirmation, nor verification that what they are expecting is ever going to happen. But they Believed, that if I hold on and keep the faith, that which I am waiting for will show up in just a little while.

And that's the problem with belief, it calls you to hold on and trust in, without absolute proof. And in this text, we are admonished to believe even in the face, no absolute proof that everything is going to work out alright. The Gospel of John is filled with irony and paradoxical circumstances with a direct focus, and intention of convincing you to recognize, understand and believe in Jesus not only as the Son of Man, but the Son of God. It calls you draws, compels you to lean in and trusts in the Son of God all based upon a word.

John is unique because all through the text, God seems to solve problems by giving people problems. Like the "light shines in darkness, but the darkness comprehended it not." God seems to solve problems by giving people problems. Like, "he came to his own

> *God seems to solve problems by giving people problems.*

people, and his own people turned their backs on him." God seems to solve problems, by giving people problems, "Like the word became flesh and started hanging out with us."

In John, the irony is overwhelming, God using problems to solve people's problems, like "quit your jobs and come and follow me." Or what about when the wine ran out and people were already feeling just about right and toasty, he goes and turns water into wine. God uses problems to solve people's problems. Or what about that one, where he told a grown man named Nicodemus, "You must be born again." God uses problems to solve people's problems. What about the one where, he tells a woman from Samaria, to go home and get the man who is not her husband, to come see another man who is not her husband, and she comes back with several men who are not her husband. God uses problems to solve people's problems. What about that day out by the Sea of Galilee, running revivals and healing services but had no money to provide a repast for the 5000 people who came to church and took a boys lunch of two fish and five loaves of bread and told his disciples to start passing it out. God uses problems to solve people's problems. You gotta believe.

In John it seems like walking with the Son of God is a walk that helps you to sometimes understand that God will use your problems to solve your problems. What about that woman was caught in adultery, as if only women could commit adultery, and her accusers brought her to Jesus to be stoned, and Jesus says, he that is without sin let him cast the first stone, and Nobody moved. Again, God uses problems to solve people's problems.

How do you lean on and rely on and believe in somebody who lets you get all the way to the end of your rope and then pulls you in? How do you trust in something that you cannot see or feel, nor touch when you need to, but every now and then opens your eyes to something you have never seen before? And every now and then, embraces you with power and understanding and whispers words of strength and encouragement in your ear. It's not because you are perfect, special or crazy, it's because you Believe.

One last story that comes into focus for this moment is the death of a friend: the death of a beloved one. The brother of Mary and Martha in our text has now been dead for days and Jesus has not come yet to see about them or to bring him back. If anybody should have gotten attention during the time of grief should have been the people whom Jesus loved and often stayed with when he was in the city of Bethany. This dead man's sister Mary, broke an expensive bottle of perfume on the feet of Jesus and he is not here yet? The dead man's sister Martha cooked for him in the soup kitchen, she was a worker, more than a worshipper, and made him meals that filled his belly, and Jesus is not here yet? We sent you a text, instagram, we posted on facebook, I emailed your disciples, I called the church, left a voicemail. The administrator said to us you got the message and you still chose to wait two more days. So what, Jesus you are going to just come whenever you get ready to come? I know they got a hit out on your life, but this is your friend, somebody you said you would be there for no matter what and now you delay coming to the grieving families side and you got the never to tell your boys, That You are glad Your Lazarus is dead, so that I can BELIEVE. (You know that got back to the family, this was Clairton, I mean Bethany, and news travels fast)

This is some crazy writing John is doing, Jesus is glad his friend is dead. Sounds like God is using problems to solve people's problems. The text tells us Jesus is two miles away in Jerusalem and Martha heard where Jesus was and left the grieving crowd and went to Jesus and said where have you Been? If you would have been here, my brother, (who is obviously more important to me than you) would not have died. And Martha also said, "But even now I know God will give you whatever you ask of him." Jesus says, He will live, and Martha says, "Yes Lord we will all get up in the resurrection, And Jesus says to her, I am The Resurrection. And now, do you believe? And Martha says, Yes Lord, I believe. Which bring out the first point:

Belief will give you access to the resource of resurrection. Martha is a Believer; A person who relies on something and does so without absolute proof that they are right in doing so. Belief will get you in some doors, that doubt will block you from every time. It has not happened yet, but it gets you in the room where anything can happen. The situation has not changed yet, but belief will get you a seat at the table where the discussion will begin to work out in your favor. Belief will give you the permission to enter into a place, a room, a situation, and in this case a confidence that you no longer have to struggle to get in. Belief says welcome, come in, sit down, and let's talk. Belief will give you a freedom, a way and a liberty to walk into what God has for you. You got to believe. Even if you don't see it now, Belief gets you close enough to it so that all you have to do is grab it when it becomes available. Martha said I know we all will get up, but Jesus said Honey, I am the GET UP. Now do you Believe? You got to Believe.

> *Belief will give you access to the resource of resurrection.*

Another lesson I think we glean from this text is also found when Jesus arrives at the grave of Lazarus, yet on the way to Calvary began to weep because of his perceived love for Lazarus. And the New Revised Standard Version of the text said, "So the Jews said, "See how he loved him." And in verse 37, "But some of them said, "Could not he who opened the eyes of the blind man have kept this man from dying?" But Jesus kept on going. I can extract here as you can also, that: Belief is going to secure you, when you are surrounded by what some of them said.

Have you ever heard the term "they said?" These are them. And you will, in life, face places and people who will always have the ability to promote doubt in the face of what you believe. And the reason you have to accept, buy and swallow, what you believe, because if you are not careful and confident, people will loudly put into question who you are and what you believe about your situation. But Jesus kept on moving. And sometimes you will have to keep on moving with no evidence and simply because you believe. You have to believe, but you also may have to ignore people.

> ## Belief will stay with you, when your stuff stinks.

In this instance Jesus keeps moving toward what he has come to do, and when he arrives at the grave, Jesus says, take the stone away. And Martha, the sister of the dead man, said to him, "Lord, there is a stench because he has been dead for four days." And Jesus says to her, "Did I not tell you, that if you believed, you would see the Glory of God." In layman's terms, Jesus is telling Martha, "Stand Down." Which may help us to understand that: Belief will stay with you, when your stuff stinks.

Even when it stinks, you have to believe. The process of decomposition has already begun in the physical body of Lazarus, and it is only natural for decomposing flesh to exert a stench or a negative smell. Now in my little research a smell does not come until a stage in the decomposition process calls Bloat, normally stage 2. By the time a body gets to stage 2, the blood has already settled because the heart has stopped pumping, and the body begins to change color. The muscles have already stiffened and gone into a process called rigor mortis. It is a place where the body becomes locked in the position it was in at the time of death. (And you trying to figure out why people don't move when the fire is burning, It's because the body becomes locked in the position). By the time the body gets to stage 2, cells have already broken down and blisters are forming on the skin and the liquids in the body begin to multiply, this is the source of bad odors. That's stage one. The odor is produced. Martha says, No Lord, There is a stench, he has been dead for 4 days. In stage 2 called bloat, the gases that were produced in stage 1 will eventually escape the body in Stage 2, so that what was hidden before becomes public knowledge to everybody else around.

And Jesus tells Martha to Stand Down, Did I not tell you that If you believe, you would see the glory. Which may help somebody in here understand when that which was private trouble becomes public stench, Belief will stay with you, when your stuff stinks. It stinks because it's natural for a dead thing to stink. But when you have made up your mind to allow God glory to be revealed, you no longer try to hide it or cover it up, you let it out so God can be glorified. And belief, confidence, assurance in something and somebody will help you STAND DOWN WHEN YOUR STUFF STINKS. You are so smelly. But Smelly is the right place for Jesus to show up and say ROLL THE STONE AWAY. Miss Ceily, said to Mister, in the movie "The Color Purple," while pulling off in the car with Shug Avery and her new husband, "I may be black, I may be ugly, but Dear God, I'm still here."

Jesus approaches the scene and tells them to roll the stone away. And sends up a prayer to his father and when he has finished, the bible says, Jesus calls out with a loud voice, "Lazarus, Come Forth."

I know your body has a stench. I know your limbs have stiffened. And you can not do what you used to do. I know your heart has stopped feeling and stopped beating, and it is callus, But Lazarus, Come Forth!

And the Bible records, the dead man came out, his hands and his feet, bound with strips of cloth, and his face wrapped in cloth. Jesus said "Unbind him and Let Him Go." And this brings out our last extraction for this message: Belief is going to prove true to you when what you believed for gets Loose.

Jesus says Loose him and let him go. Your belief is going to prove true, because what you believed for is going to come through. At one point you believed it, but now you are going to see it. You held on when you had nothing to hold on to, but God is getting ready to roll the stone away and call your Lazarus to Come Forth. And the same people that tied and wrapped it up are going to be the same people that God is going to instruct, Loose him and let him go.

But you got to believe, it just might be your belief that brings you out. It just might be your belief that brings you over. It just might be your belief that brings you through. It just might be your belief that saves your family. It just might be your belief that changes your community. It just might be your belief that saves your church. You got to believe.

> John 1:12 But as many as received him, to them gave him power to become the sons of God, even to those that believe in his name.

> John 3:15 That whosoever believeth in him should not perish, but have eternal life.

> John 7:38 He that believeth on me, as the scripture hath said, out of his belly shall flow rivers of living water.

> John 11:27 Martha unto him, Yea, Lord: I believe that thou art the Christ, the Son of God, which should come into the world.

And Martha gives us the pattern and says "You Got to Believe."

I Am God's Masterpiece.

Well Here Goes, "I Believe." I believe in God the Father, God the Son, and God the Holy Spirit.

I believe God, the Creator of all things, loves me so much that through faith in his Son, Jesus Christ, all my sins are forgiven and I have eternal life. I believe Jesus was born in Africa of a virgin birth, and after his death he rose to reign with God and now intercedes with God on my behalf. I believe God, through the Holy Spirit, resides in me and gives me power in all my circumstances. I believe the kingdom of God is within each of us. I do not have to wait until death to enjoy the presence of God. I believe I am unique and made in the image of God to reflect God's likeness. I believe I am fearfully and wonderfully made. I am God's masterpiece.

I believe God desires me to be healthy and whole. God orchestrates events in my life to cause me to prosper and succeed. I believe God causes all things that happen to work for the good for those who love the Lord and are called according to God's purpose. I believe God appoints angels to watch over God's people. I believe through faith I can do all things. Nothing is impossible for those who believe.

It's Revival, But You Got To Believe.

-SEVEN-

Many saints resurrected at Jesus' crucifixion

Matthew 27:52-53 (KJV)

52 And the graves were opened; and many bodies of the saints which slept arose,

53 And came out of the graves after his resurrection, and went into the holy city, and appeared unto many.

Don't Get Stuck At the Cross   Rev. John H. Gamble Jr.

The Resurrection of Jesus Christ

Matthew 27:50-54

Lavonn Brown, in "The Other Half of the Rainbow," gives an interesting illustration about how people view the death of Christ. He says,

> Every year, thousands of people climb a mountain in the Italian Alps, passing the "stations of the cross" to stand at an outdoor crucifix. One tourist noticed a little trail that led beyond the cross. He fought through the rough thicket and, to his surprise, came upon another shrine, a shrine that symbolized the empty tomb. It was neglected. The brush had grown up around it. Almost everyone had gone as far as the cross, but there they stopped.

> (His point?) Far too many have gotten to the cross and have known the despair and the heart break (of the death of Christ). Far too few have moved beyond the cross to find the real message of Easter, which is the newness of life.

Don't get stuck at the cross! And I think that this is an important message because too many of us think that it was the cross alone that made the difference. We make the mistake of putting all our emphasis on the cross, when there is more to the story than just the cross. Don't get me wrong! I thank God for the cross. Thank God that on that Friday, he died! But Good Friday wouldn't have been so good, if there wasn't for an early Sunday morning!

You know the story! Early on Sunday morning, as the new day was dawning, Mary Magdalene and the other Mary went out to see the tomb. Suddenly there was a great earthquake. An angel of the Lord came down from heaven, rolled away the stone and sat on it. The guards shook with fear and fell out when they saw him. Then the angel spoke to the women and said, "Don't be afraid! I know you are looking for Jesus, who was crucified. He isn't here; for He has risen just as he said. Come and see the place where his body once laid." And when the women saw the empty tomb and Jesus wasn't there, the angel said, "Now go tell the disciples!"

In other words, children of God, our testimony is about more than the Cross. Our testimony is about more than the fact that he died. Our testimony is about the fact that He lives! We can't get stuck at the Cross, because if we get stuck at the Cross, then we only tell part of the story. And the message of salvation is not just that He died, but message of salvation is that He rose again! That why Paul says, 1 Corinthians 15,

> If Christ be not risen, then is our preaching vain, and your faith is also vain… we are false witnesses of God; because we have testified that God raised up Christ… If Christ be not raised, your faith is vain and we are yet in your sins; and those who have fallen asleep in Christ will perish!

And so in the text, Matthew 27, the death of Jesus is recorded. Matthew, the writer of this gospel, focuses his attention toward writing about Jesus, as the second Moses, the greatest of the prophets, who is more than a prophet. He is prophet, priest, and King. In the story of his death, Matthew records how a murderer is freed, while Jesus is judged. Pilate says he is innocent, but the crowd declared him guilty. He is beaten and scourged. They twist a crown of thorns on his head, throw a red robe on his body, spit on him, and laugh as they declare him king of the Jews. They force him to carry his own cross down the streets of Jerusalem and when he can't carry the cross any further, they grab a man (Simon of Cyrene) out of the crowd to carry the cross the rest of the way.

And when they get up Calvary's hill, to the place of the skull (Golgotha), they strip him down, impale him to the cross. They try to make him drink poison, cast lots for his clothes, and the mock him saying, "If you are who you say you are, if you are the Son of God, come down from the Cross!"

And we know that on the Cross, Jesus makes seven statements on the Cross, and after he speaks for the last time, the Bible says that he yielded up his spirit. Traditional King James says, "He gave up the ghost!" In other words, Jesus died. But if we get stuck at the Cross, we might miss the significance of what the resurrection is all about. So right at the point of Jesus' death, God saw fit to make some things happen so that we would understand that the Cross is not the end of the story. The Bible says, (verse 51),

> *51 Then, behold, the veil of the temple was torn in two from top to bottom; and the earth quaked, and the rocks were split, 52 and the graves were opened; and many bodies of the saints who had fallen asleep were raised; 53 and coming out of the graves after His resurrection, they went into the holy city and appeared to many. 54 So when the centurion and those with him, who were guarding Jesus, saw the earthquake and the things that had happened, they feared greatly, saying, "Truly this was the Son of God!"*

Don't miss it! Three things happen right at the moment of Christ's death to show us that this is not the end of the story. The veil is torn. The earth is shaken. AND the graves are opened!

And if we look at each one of those, we understand why we can't get stuck at the Cross. First, veil was torn. As a matter of fact, it says that the veil was torn from the top to the bottom. This veil was the entrance to the Most Holy Place where it was believed that the presence of God dwelt among the people. According to the writings of Josephus, the Jewish historian, the veil was four inches thick and horses tied to each side could not pull the veil apart. But when Jesus died, the veil split in two!

And you won't understand the power of the text if you don't understand what happened behind the veil. The temple was divided into sections, and depending on your status determined where you stood in the temple. If you were not Jewish, you stood in the Court of the Gentiles. If you were a Jewish women, you could move a little closer into the women's court. If you were a Jewish man, you could get closer than the women and stand in the court of Israel. If you were a priest, you could get even closer and stand in the priestly court. But only the High Priest stood at the altar, and would offer the sacrifice. He was privileged to go from the inner sanctuary into the Holy of Holies/Most Holy Place to bring the sacrifice for the Lord. In other words, gentiles couldn't sacrifice for themselves. Jewish women couldn't sacrifice for themselves. Even the men and the priest couldn't sacrifice for themselves. Everything was contingent on there being a high priest to go to God on their behalf. But because of Jesus, the veil is torn, never to be replaced. His sacrifice, the shedding of His own blood, was a sufficient, once and for all atonement for our sins.

It's like the little boy who broke the preacher's umbrella. The son of Cyrus McCormick was 11 years old when he met D. L. Moody. D. L. Moody was visiting his father and had left his shoulder bag and umbrella at the house. The boy was asked to walk over to get the bag and the umbrella for him. Carrying the items, he placed the satchel on the end of the umbrella and he had the umbrella poised over my shoulder. He then tripped and fell, breaking the umbrella! He was upset and afraid that D. L. Moody would be upset with him. So, he thought, "I will tell mother;

she can tell father, and father can tell Mr. Moody." So, he hurried home and told mother. The mother told the father; and father broke the news to D.L. Moody. D.L. Moody went to the boy and said. "When you broke my umbrella, you became frightened and ashamed, didn't you? Then you thought. If I tell mother or father, they can go between me and Mr. Moody and straighten things up. Now that your father has straightened things up, you can come to me. Now, my lad, that is the way it is with all of us; we are sinners—afraid of God. But God has provided a Mediator—someone to go between us and Him—and it is Jesus!"

And that's why you can't get stuck at the Cross, because if you get stuck at the Cross, you won't bring the broken things in your life to God! The veil in the temple was a constant reminder that sin made us unfit for the presence of God. Jesus Christ, through His death, has removed the veil, the barrier between God and man, and now we may approach God with confidence and boldness, even in our brokenness. And I don't know about you, but there are some things in my life that are broken, that I need to bring before the Lord. There are some sins I have committed that I need to bring before the Lord. There are some issues I have that I need to bring before the Lord. And because I know that the cross is not the end of the story, and he lives, I know that whatever I'm going through I can take it to the Lord. Because whatever I am dealing with, Jesus dealt with it so I can have victory over it! Hebrews 4:15,

> *15 For we have not an high priest which cannot be touched with the feeling of our infirmities; but was in all points tempted like as we are, yet without sin.16 Let us therefore come boldly unto the throne of grace, that we may obtain mercy, and find grace to help in time of need.*

Paul says, (1 Timothy 2:5-6),

5 For there is one God and one mediator between God and men, the
man Christ Jesus, who gave himself as a ransom for all men.

All I'm trying to tell you is if you get stuck at the Cross, you will think
that you have to wait for somebody else to go to God for you, when you
can go to God for yourself!

(You need to have your own prayer life. You need to have your own
conversations with the Lord. Don't trust folks to bring your situation to
God. They might bring it to everybody BUT God! You better learn how
to bring it to God yourself. Say your own prayer. Have your own talk
with Jesus! The veil is torn! Nobody can talk to God about your situation
better than you!

That's why the old church would say, "Jesus is on the main line, tell him
what you want!")

The veil is torn, which means we have unlimited access to God. But then,
the Bible says, that the earth was shaken. In other words, Christ died and
there was an earthquake. And while there are several examples, both
implicitly and explicitly, in the scripture where there was an earthquake,
I noticed that whenever there was an earthquake during a time of distress,
God spoke.

Exodus chapter 19, the people are complaining in the wilderness. All
manner of issues are arising, to where judges have to be placed about the
children of Israel to settle their disputes. The Bible says,

17 Then Moses led the people out of the camp to meet with God, and
they stood at the foot of the mountain.18 Mount Sinai was covered
with smoke, because the LORD descended on it in fire. The smoke
billowed up from it like smoke from a furnace, the whole mountain

trembled violently, 19 and the sound of the trumpet grew louder and louder. Then Moses spoke and the voice of God answered him.

Elijah runs from Ahab and Jezebel. Sits up under a juniper tree, ready to die. God sustains him. He goes and stands upon the mountain before the LORD. The LORD passed by, and a strong wind and breaks the rocks into pieces but the LORD was not in the wind: and after the wind an earthquake; but the LORD was not in the earthquake: And after the earthquake a fire; but the LORD was not in the fire: and after the fire, there was a still small voice. And when Elijah heard it, he wrapped his face in his mantle, went out, and stood in the entrance of the cave. The Lord spoke to Elijah!

Don't miss the message. Here Jesus has died on the cross, but the earth is still shaking. The first earthquake occurred in creation, when the dry land appeared. But this earthquake occurs in redemption. The earthquake in the text is a reminder that, even in your darkest moments, God is still speaking. Even in your darkest moments, God is still in control.

And somebody in this building today, you need to understand that the resurrection is about the fact God controls everything even life and death. You see, at the cross, they thought they were killing Christ. At the cross, they thought they were getting rid of Him. But they weren't listening. Jesus said, (John 10:17)

> I lay down my life, that I might take it again. No man takes it from me, but I lay it down of myself. I have power to lay it down, and I have power to take it again.

That's what we need to remember. That God is in control! You can't give up. You can't throw in the towel. You can't call it quits. Because even in your darkest moments, God is still in control!

Isn't that what the disciples learn in the midst of a raging sea? The storm comes. The earth shakes. The winds and waves beat against the ship. Jesus is at the bottom of the boat sleep. You know the story…. Jesus says, "Peace, be still!"…

No matter how dark the situation is, God is still in control.

The veil is torn (unlimited access). The earth is shaken (ultimate authority). But then it says that the graves are opened (undeserved awakening). The Bible says,

> *52 and the graves were opened; and many bodies of the saints who had fallen asleep were raised; 53 and coming out of the graves after His resurrection, they went into the holy city and appeared to many.*

Don't miss what happens in the text. The saints of the Old Testament were long dead. In the Jewish tradition, the belief was that the dead went to a silent, yet eternal, resting place called Sheol. It was the place of death. The belief was that when you went to Sheol; that was it. There was no life. It was the place from which there is no resurrection. But the Bible says that the graves opened. Now the saints didn't come out until after he got up, but the point is that the graves were opened, which means that in Christ there is always potential for a person to rise again. In other words, in Christ, it's not over until God says, it's over. Let me see if I can help you.

IN OCTOBER of 1987, a little girl named Jessica McClure fell down an abandoned well shaft. The shaft was eight inches in diameter and twenty-two feet deep. She was lost to her parents with no way on her own to get out. She was trapped. In this little town of Midland, Texas, she became the focus of the whole nation. Every major news network focused on Midland, Texas, and the girl named Jessica, who was trapped in the well.

For fifteen hours, men dug and drilled. They didn't know initially that to get to her they would have to go through some limestone. This stone cracked the bits on the drills they were using to make their way through the shaft. Getting to little Jessica took a lot longer than anyone expected. After fifteen hours or so someone was able to get down into the shaft, untangle little Jessica, and bring her up to the top. Cameras blazing upon the opening to the shaft caught the man bringing Jessica up out of the shaft and into the arms of her waiting parents. The site, filled with people hoping and praying, was filled with joy. The rescuers were crying, the parents were crying, newscasters were crying, and onlookers across the nation were crying because little Jessica, who was most certainly dead, was now alive. Little Jessica, in order to live, had to have somebody else save her.

(From Tony Evans) Just like Jessica, sin had us trapped. We fall into holes we can't lift ourselves out of. If we want to get out of the hole, somebody up there has got to come down to where we've been trapped. Somebody has got to drill a hole to where we are.

That's what Jesus did. He saw you and me in a hole. We were trying to get out with good works, but we weren't getting anywhere. But God, coming as the person of Jesus Christ, entered the hole of our death, and offered deliverance from above!

And that's why we can't stay at the cross, because they open graves suggest that whatever we are in that is holding us... has us bound... that is keeping us down, through Christ we have power to live!

> *Regardless of where you are in life, if you understand who Jesus is, the same way Jesus rose, we can rise up!*

And somebody in the building ought to thank God that it wasn't too late. Regardless of where you are in life, if you understand who Jesus is, the same way Jesus rose, we can rise up!

That's why I don't allow everybody to speak into my life. I don't allow some people to talk to me… give me advice... go to everyone for spiritual counseling, because some people will keep you in the grave, when God is expecting you to come out of the grave! That was the power of what happened in the grave. Nobody expected the saints to show up again in Jerusalem. Nobody expected them to live again. And if people didn't expect the best of the best to get up, then there are a whole lot of people counting you out to. But thank God that my faith and my fate is not determine by people; my life is in the hands of the Lord. Thank God that I'm in his hands.

(CLOSE) you see, because of what happened right after the Cross, you can't get stuck at the Cross!

You see, the veil is torn to show we have unlimited access to God. The earth is shaken to show us the ultimate authority of God. The graves are opened showing us that, in Christ, there is an underserved awakening by God.

And as a result, there is an unexpected affirmation of God. For the Bible says,

54 So when the centurion and those with him, who were guarding Jesus, saw the earthquake and the things that had happened, they feared greatly, saying, "Truly this was the Son of God!"

The Centurion was a roman soldier. He was polytheistic. He believed in many gods, but after seeing what the happened after the cross, he confessed, "Surely this must be the Son of God!"

And that's where I want to close, because it was not the Cross, that demonstrated his power; it was what happened after the Cross!

It's the cross that redeemed us, but it was the empty tomb that saved us! And when people can see the change that comes in those of us who believe that Christ is not dead, but he has risen just as he said, there will be no choice but to confess that Jesus is the Son of God!

And I don't know about you, but I am not stuck at the cross! Because what I am experiencing God in my life right now.

I am glad for the cross, but I thank God for what He is doing right now.

He blessed me then, but He is blessing me right now!

The Proof of Revival   Dr. Willie J. Thompson Jr.

Matthew 27:45, 52-53 (KJV)

45 At noon, darkness fell across the whole land until three o'clock. 46 At about three o'clock, Jesus called out with a loud voice, "Eli, Eli, lema sabachthani?" which means "My God, my God, why have you abandoned me?" 47 Some of the bystanders misunderstood and thought he was calling for the prophet Elijah. 48 One of them ran and filled a sponge with sour wine, holding it up to him on a reed stick so he could drink. 49 But the rest said, "Wait! Let's see whether Elijah comes to save him." 50 Then Jesus shouted out again, and he released his spirit. 51 At that moment the curtain in the sanctuary of the Temple was torn in two, from top to bottom. The earth shook, rocks split apart,

52 and tombs opened. The bodies of many godly men and women who had died were raised from the dead. 53 They left the cemetery after Jesus' resurrection, went into the holy city of Jerusalem, and appeared to many people.

54 The Roman officer and the other soldiers at the crucifixion were terrified by the earthquake and all that had happened. They said, "This man truly was the Son of God!" 55 And many women who had come from Galilee with Jesus to care for him were watching from a distance. 56 Among them were Mary Magdalene, Mary (the mother of James and Joseph), and the mother of James and John, the sons of Zebedee.

Matthew's Gospel is the bridge that leads us out of the Old Testament and into the New Testament. The Old Testament is a book of promise while the New Testament is a book of fulfillment. While the Old Testament tells us something is on the way, the New Testament handles the business. While the Old Testament points us towards a future glory, the New Testament executes the order. While the Old Testament tells us, the New Testament shows us what we were looking for. And Matthew's Gospel is the bridge, it is the passage, the pontoon and catwalk that takes us from pledge to perfection. And takes us from commitment to carrying out. And it takes us from agreement to achievement.

If you are one, that was promised something and have been in expectation of the promise to make good on a promise, just open Matthew's Gospel, open his good news of the kingdom and let it become the bridge that will take you right on over into what you have been waiting for. You had a picture of it, but open this Gospel and see it. You imagined it, but open this gospel and hold it in your hand. Today is the day you no longer shout because it is coming, today you shout because it is HERE.

In Matthew, Jesus becomes the fulfillment of the Old Testament promise. He is the evidence that what was promised, will come to pass. He is the vow kept and the contract carried through. Jesus is the evidence that God will keep his Word to His people. In Genesis (3:15) God promised a redeemer and when Jesus shows up in Matthew that promised if fulfilled. In Isaiah (7:14) the promise that a virgin will conceive a son and that promise fulfilled in Matthew (1:22-23) when she gave birth and called him Immanuel. In Hosea (11:1) the child was called out of Egypt, and in Matthew (2:14-15) Jesus was taken to Egypt for safety fulfilling that promise. Matthew wrote just to make sure that the Jews and Gentiles of that day and the believers of this day, know beyond that if God promised it, God will pay it, and if God consented to it God will carry it through. And the fulfillment is the evidence of what was promised.

If we keep it one hundred, you can't stand when people promise you something and they don't keep their promise. You can't stand when people give you their word about something and they do not do what they say. But aren't you glad that even when people don't keep their word, God still keeps His word. And the fulfillment is the proof and the evidence of what was promised.

> *If we keep it one hundred, you can't stand when people promise you something and they don't keep their promise.*

When a man suddenly appears and claims to be the king, the messiah, the awaited one and the promised ruler, the public immediately asks for proof. Matthew gives a detailed account of the life and teachings of Jesus as proof of His Messiahship. He presents that He came through human and divine heredity. He came through people who needed grace and through one who could extend grace. His arrival was herald by three kings, and he was the anointed King of Kings. Jesus grew up in Nazareth and carried the credential of a carpenter. Jesus had a cousin named John the Baptist, who said there is one that comes after me whose shoes I am not worthy to untie, and one day saw Him and said, "Behold the Lamb of God which taketh away the sins of the world;" evidence, proof, of a promise extended in one dispensation of time and fulfilled in another.

If you are, who you say you are Jesus, where is the proof? Where is the evidence? Matthew introduces the person of the King, and Matthew presents the principles of the King, but what we are after in this season of revival, is the Power of the King. Afterall, if a king does not have the power to accomplish anything, what good are his credentials and principles? What can you do sir that gives us proof and some evidence that you are who you say you are?

Now in Matthew (8-9) there were a few miracles that gave evidence that Jesus had power: he healed the leper, the centurion's servant and Peter's mother-in-law. He stepped out and calmed the storm over the Sea of Galilee. He brought peace to the sin-sick and wandering soul. He had power that not only served as evidence but it also brought weight to his ministry and message. Jesus was a fulfilled promise, but even as a fulfilled promise, the King also had conflict, concerns and in today's text a cross.

Matthew records that the proof, and evidence was mocked by soldiers. The evidence and proof was given over to a capital punishment method called crucifixion. The evidence was mocked not only by strangers but also by the very people he came to save and executed on a public highway. In the focal passage it was 9 o'clock in the morning and from 9 until noon, the proof and evidence hung in the light. But at noon a miraculous darkness covered the land. According to theologians, it was not an eclipse, it was a heaven sent darkness that lasted for three hours. It was as if all of creation was sympathizing with the Creator. The Bible says about the ninth hour Jesus cries out with a loud voice, saying, Eli, Eli, lema sabachthani?"He spoke in Hebrew and the people watching thought he was calling for Elijah to help him. The evidence and proof said three more things and when He got ready, they didn't force him, when he got ready, he said, It is Finished. He gave up the Ghost. And verse 50 says, "He died."

Theologians suggest that three miracles took place simultaneously: One, the veil of the temple was torn in two from top to bottom, two, an earthquake shook the earth and shook open many graves and three, SOME saints arose from the dead. Now they tell me the rending of the veil was the proof and the evidence that the way for us to get to God was open. There was no need for that old sacrificial system. Jesus has just finished the hard part on the cross. They tell me that the earthquake at Calvary was proof that demands of the Law had been met and that the curse of the Law has been abolished, destroyed and nullified. When the earth shook, that is proof and evidence that the curse has been lifted, repealed and rescinded.

But I think I found a few proofs of my own, when the graves opened up and the Saints who were asleep in death, got up and began to walk the streets of the holy city showing themselves to many. I think I have found evidence of what provokes revival.

I raise the chief concern; "Why does the death of Jesus provoke revival for the Saints?

In verse 51-52, the text says, "after the death of Jesus, the earth shook and rocks were split and graves opened up." I would like to suggest that this is proof that "Too many graves thought they had the victory."

> *"Too many graves thought they had the victory."*

Now a grave is any place that becomes the receptacle of what is dead, lost or past. And if the Greek translation of the word is correct, the text is saying graces or monuments opened up. And monuments are reminders of what we have done. And monuments are witnesses to what happened in our past and monuments are mementos of our yesterdays. And sometimes we can get stuck in our past, and stuck in where we have been and what we have gone through. But monuments can also be good things that we have done, and now we are blocked from moving forward because we keep celebrating the good ole days.

We sometimes relish what we have done, and when we do that we make a monument out of something that was supposed to serve a purpose for that time. And when we get stuck, the veil rips in twain, the earth begins to shake and the tombs begin to speak, because too many of them testify to what was and can be blocking us from getting to where God wants us to be. The death of Jesus provokes revival for the saints, because too many reminders of our past have been allowed to have the final say. But when the tombs are opened wide it is evidence that Jesus has not only overcome death, but he has also overcome the grave. Your past mistakes or accomplishments are not as important as your future reality. And when you let your past be your past, you provide evidence that Revival has come to your life. Don't you let what you did have the final say. If you are still here, God has more for you to do. Move Forward. Don't allow the receptacle of dead things, lost things and past things to have the victory and final say. Move Forward.

Not only did too many graves think they had the victory, But verse 52, also lets us know that, not only did, "the graves opened, but many bodies of the saints who had fallen asleep were raised." My chief concern is "Why does the death of Jesus provoke revival of the Saints, I would like to suggest that this is proof that, "There were too many of God's men and women that had fallen asleep." Now the passive or reflexive meaning of the word "sleep," means "to sleep," shut your eyes and go to sleep. (Not now in the sermon, but when it is time, later on). But the figurative meaning of the word means to decrease, become common, defiled, polluted, unclean and deflated. Could it be that the Saints in the text were sleeping, But also for us, could it be necessary for Jesus to die and send revival, because the Saints in the pews have become common, defiled, polluted, unclean and simply deflated? Have we allowed the things of this world to take out our air, or our wind, that makes us useful to the Kingdom of God. How many of the men and women of God have fallen asleep? When hate comes we have no air? When racism comes, we have no air? When domestic violence comes we have no air. When poverty and injustice comes we have no air? When disease comes we have no air. Have we, the Saints of God become common, unclean and empty, no longer desiring the WIND AND POWER of the HOLY GHOST? Revival had to come. The text records the veil ripped in two, the earth shook, the graves did not have the final say and many of the Saints were brought back to life. Jesus had to die so that the believers could live and not just by power, or by might, But the believer must live by the SPIRIT, the WIND, NEUMA And Breath of God. Jesus died and many of the SAINTS came back to life. Revival struck out in the graveyard, and if God can do it for Dead believers, what do you think you can do with you? You are still walking around in the land of the living and not of the dead. If God can stop the death process and make dead Saints get up, won't he do the same for you and your situation. The death of Jesus provoked the revival of the Saints, because too many of them were asleep. WAKE UP. Revival comes to wake you up if you are asleep. Revival comes to stand you up if you have been knocked down. Revival comes to heal you if you have been sick. Revival comes to build you where you have been torn down. Revival comes to restore what has been taken. The wind of God is in you. The breath of God fills you, now say what God has told you to say.

The death of Jesus provokes the revival of the Saints, not only because too many graves thought they had the victory, and not only because too many of God's servants had fallen asleep, but lastly I would like to suggest, according to verse 53, that says after the resurrection of Christ, the Saints that were in opened graves, came out of the graves came out of the graves, went in to the Holy city and showed themselves to many, and that is proof, that, "There were too many people in God's city that still didn't believe."

> "There were too many people in God's city that still didn't believe."

The Saints that were raised and given breath, did not just go anywhere and everywhere the text specifically says, they got up and went into the Holy City and showed themselves to many. The Saints went to places that were dedicated to God. The Saints went to people who were dedicated to God. Which is evidence and proof for us, that you can be in God's city and you can be in God's church and you can be in God's house and still not believe. Survey research says that more than 53% of people who grew up in church, when they reach adult age, will deny the church of their rearing. And begin to use the word spiritual instead or born again, blood washed, and holy ghost filled. See you can be in the church and the church not be in you. The Saints had to get up from their graves when Jesus died, because there were too many people in God's city that did not believe. There were too many people in God's dwelling that saw his miracles, but did not believe. There were too many people that saw what he did for their neighbor, and still not believe. There were too many people that saw how he saved their children from accidents and drug addictions and turned them around but still did not believe. They had to get up from the gardens they were in, they had to get up from the roadside cemeteries they were in because too many people in God's city did not believe. Jesus' death is connected to the revival of the Saints, because there were too many people in God's city, walking God's streets, eating God's food, enjoying God's creations, hearing God's laws, praising God's name, who did not believe Jesus was who he said he was. All I'm trying to say is, if you are going to be in his house, you might as well believe in who he is.

Matthew says, "His name is Emmanuel, Do you Believe it?" (1:23)

Matthew says, "He is the Son of David, Do you Believe it?" (9:27)

Matthew says, "He is called King, Do you Believe it?" (1:23)

Matthew says, "He is the Christ, the Son of the Living God, Do you Believe it?" (16:16)

Don't sit in his house and not believe on His name.

Mark says, "He is the Son of God, Do you Believe it?" (9:7)

Luke says He is the King of the Jews." (23:36-37) "Do you believe It?

John says He is, "The Bread of Life," (6:35) "Do you believe It?

Acts says, He is "The Holy One, (3:14) "Do you believe It?

Romans says, He is "The Deliverer," (11:26) "Do you believe It?

Corinthians says, He is "The Passover Lamb," (5:7) "Do you believe It?

Galatians says He is "Abraham's Seed," (3:16) "Do you believe It?

Ephesians says, He is "The Head Over All Things, (4:23) "Do you believe It?

Phillipians, says He gives me power to do all things," (1:2)

Colossians says, He is "God's Mystery (2:2) "Do you believe It?

Thessalonians says, He is the silent tongue that breathes no threats and minds his own business (4:11-12) "Do you believe It?

Timothy says, He is "God the Father," (1:2) Do you believe it?

Philemon says, He is a gracious God (1:25) Do you believe it?

Hebrews calls him the Apostle and High Priest (3:1) Do you believe it?

James says He is the Generous God (1:5) Do you Believe it?

Peter says, He is the Chief Shepherd, and Shepherd over all Shepherds (5:4) Do you believe it?

1st , 2nd & 3rd John says, He is "The Son of The Father, and Only Begotten of God (1:3 & 18) Do you believe it?

Jude says He is Jesus Christ (1:1) Do you believe it?

Revelation says He is the Faithful Witness (1:5) Do you Believe it?

Revelation says He is the Lion of Judah (5:5) Do you Believe it?

Revelation says He is the Bright and Morning Star (22:16) Do you Believe it?

Jesus had to die, so that revival could come to the saints, because so many people were around that didn't believe.

But one more verse tells us, That there was one, who did not need to get back to the city. But he was right there at the foot of the cross. He helped put the nails in his hands. He helped put the nails in His feet. He probably was the one that gave him vinegar to drink, when he was thirsty. He probably was the one that cast lots for the clothes of Jesus and had a souvenir to take home for his kids. He saw the sky go dark. He saw the moon drip away in blood, he felt the earthquake shake the earth. He saw rocks split. He saw the tombs open up. He felt the rumbling and the rolling. He started to tremble and shake and fear gripped him. He was guilty, he participated in the death of the Lord Jesus, he fell to his knees and looked up at the body of Jesus, and was totally convinced and said surely, this man was the son of God.

And somebody in the room, you've seen the lighting flashing, you have heard the thunder rolling, you have felt sin breakers dashing, trying to conquer your soul. But today can you hear Jesus say Fight on. He will never leave you alone. And knowing this will give you the evidence, and the proof that you need to provoke revival to break out in your life. WAKE UP, It's Revival.

-EIGHT-

A Christ's Resurrection

Matthew 28:5-7 (KJV)

5 And the angel answered and said unto the women, Fear not ye: for I know that ye seek Jesus, which was crucified.

6 He is not here: for he is risen, as he said. Come, see the place where the Lord lay.

7 And go quickly, and tell his disciples that he is risen from the dead; and, behold, he goeth before you into Galilee; there shall ye see him: lo, I have told you.

"Good News From The Grave"   Dr. Willie J. Thompson Jr.

Matthew 28:1-10

Early on Sunday morning, as the new day was dawning, Mary Magdalene and the other Mary came to see the grave. 2 Suddenly there was a great earthquake; for an angel of the Lord came down from heaven and rolled aside the stone and sat on it. 3 His face shone like lightning and his clothing was a brilliant white. 4 The guards shook with fear when they saw him, and fell into a dead faint. 5 Then the angel spoke to the women. "Don't be frightened!" he said. "I know you are looking for Jesus, who was crucified, 6 but he isn't here! For he has come back to life again, just as he said he would. Come in and see where his body was lying. . . . 7 And now, go quickly and tell his disciples that he has risen from the dead, and that he is going to Galilee to meet them there. That is my message to them."

8 They went away from the grave in a hurry. They were afraid and yet had much joy. They ran to tell the news to His followers.

9 And as they were running, suddenly Jesus was there in front of them! "Good morning!" he said. And they fell to the ground before him, holding his feet and worshiping him. 10 Then Jesus said to them, "Don't be frightened! Go tell my brothers to leave at once for Galilee, to meet me there."

Good News From The Grave

Most people turn to various platforms to get local information and news about their community. And according to some research, depending on the subject matter, most people have and use several means to catch up on the latest news, rumors, scandal, hearsay, the low down and word, out on the streets.

People today use newspapers as a top source for news on community events, crime, local government, social services, zoning and development. People today use television as a source of weather and breaking news, the latest info on politicians and traffic.

People use the internet as the top source for information about restaurants and other local businesses. And surf the web for information on housing, schools, jobs and references for the best company. They use media outlets like "Angie's List," to find out if they should use a business or not. They go to "Rate my professor.com" to see if they should take a professor or not for an academic course.

And yes, people even still use the radio as the top source for in-time information on traffic. What's going on in American or social culture, but more so to jam on the way to work, play or church. People always have ways of getting information, the 4-1-1, the tidings and headlines about whatever it is that they want to know about.

Even in small communities, people have ways of getting the news or information that they need to be informed about their surroundings. When I was a child, the guy who wanted to know or date my older sister came by the house. My grandfather did not go to e-harmony.dot com., Black people meet.dot com, or match dot com. To find out where he had come from. He sat him down in the living room and said "Boy, Who Your People."

> *In every community, there is always somebody in that community that knows everything they don't need to know.*

And not just the good, helpful, information but also the unnecessary and messy information finds its way into the ear and sensory preceptors of peoples inquiry. In every community, there is always somebody in that community that knows everything they don't need to know. And if they know it, they don't need to tell it. You do good and it spreads slowly, but you let your good step slip, and bad news will travel faster than a 747, on the Pittsburgh International Runway. People have ways of getting the news about whatever it is that they want to know.

But in this particular text, the writer of Matthew's gospel understands his audience, and they are interested in information. They want to know "Who is this Jesus," this Son of God, who came to save humanity from sin. They wanted the news. And Matthew does just that. He gives them the real-time eyewitness news in the streets of Jerusalem. Can't you just hear the street talk?

Headline: Jesus has a lineage that stretches back for 42 generations, which include Father Abraham, Isaac and Jacob, but also David, the murderer and Rahab the Harlot. Can't you just hear the street talk?

Headline: Jesus is the Son of a carpenter named Joseph, whom we see everyday, but when he prays, he says "Our Father Who Art in Heaven." Can't you just hear the street talk?

Headline: The angels call him the Prince of Peace, but down in the cut, they say he's turning sons against their fathers, and daughters against their mothers. Can't you just hear the street talk?

Headline: Jesus' cousin, John The Baptist gets killed, and Jesus missed the funeral because he was feeding 5000 with two fish and five loaves of bread. Can't you just hear the street talk?

Headline: Jesus, the Self-Proclaimed King, enters the city, not in a Rose Royce. Not in a Bentley. But this king came in on a donkey and colt while the crowds yelled out, "Hosanna to the Son of David." Can't you just hear the street talk?

Matthew presents the news. Juicy Jerusalem News.com; Jesus' right hand man denies knowing him. Jesus' financial secretary sells him out for 30 pieces of silver. Headline: Jesus to stand trial in the middle of the night. Jesus was charged with blasphemy and sentenced to death. News Flash: The Jesus administration, financial secretary, is found hung in Blood Field. Jerusalem Twitter reports: Jesus carries a cross up Golgotha's hill. Centurion Soldiers Instagram account just posted: Jesus is executed in cold blood, and then he updated saying, "Surely this was the Son of God." Jesus is placed in a borrowed tomb. And the noise and the news, the tabloids all cease. But there was one more story that needed to be told, and it could only come from the grave.

So Matthew puts on his coat and hat, and grabs a pen and pencil and runs to get a front row seat. Looking for a lead to a fresh story in a dead place. Can you imagine what would have been said if he told people where he was going to get his next story. Could you imagine what rumors would have been spread around town, before he got back, If he told people where he was going to get the next installment of news for the information purposes of the people.

> *No one looks for the latest updates of life and destiny and direction for your future in a graveyard.*

No one thinks to look for information in the graveyard? No one looks for the latest updates of life and destiny and direction for your future in a graveyard. That's the end of the story. Not the next reel. That's the place of the dead. That's the place where bodies are decomposing. That's the place where those who lived stopped. That's the place where dreams have been deferred and some even canceled.

Who would have ever thought to use the place of pain and despair and anguish for some folks as a place to find some good news? Ain't nobody trying to hang out in the graveyard for the latest gossip. Don't you know what happens in the graveyard at night? Don't you know its ghost in the graveyard? Nobody's moving in the graveyard, nobody's talking in the graveyard and who in their right mind goes to a graveyard to get some news. And some breaking news at that.

But did you know that one of the chief sources of information on ancient, prehistoric culture and numerous archaeological cultures is found in the graveyard?

And actually out of all the news that has been presented, the best news for the believer is found in this story right here. Here are the details:

Early Sunday morning, just before the break of Day. Mary the mother of Jesus and the other Mary went to the tomb of Jesus. Suddenly there was a great earthquake, because the Angel of the Lord descended from heaven and went ahead of the two on their way to the tomb. His face was like lightning, and he must have had a lot of muscles, because by the time they got there the stone was rolled away. And we don't know for sure but he must have said something pretty important, because the two guards laid out like dead men presumably from the shock of the angel's appearance.

And the angel told the women, "Fear Not" for I know you seek Jesus who was crucified. He is not here, for he has risen as he said. And there it is right there. Matthew shares with us the "Good news from the grave," that this scene left for our information by Jesus himself. And Jesus tells us: "That sometimes you have to announce your own resurrection."

The angel says, "He is not here, for he has risen as he said." Didn't Jesus tell them, if you tear down this tabernacle, in three days, I will raise it up again. He announced his own resurrection. And sometimes in this life, when you see stuff coming, even if you don't know if you are going to make it through it, you are gonna have to learn how to announce your own come back.

Do you remember the 1984 science fiction film "The Terminator," whereas a cyber assassin played by Arnold Schwarzenegger, is trying to get to Sarah Conner, but she is being housed in a heavily occupied police station and Schwarzenegger is outnumbered. In this instance, knowing he is outnumbered, under-resourced, and in over his head announces to the guard, I'll Be Back. And here in this text, Jesus was out numbered, and under-resourced and visibly in a deep dead situation. But before he got there, He said "I'll be back." And here his word proves true and that's Good News from the grave. So when you are outnumbered, under-resourced and in over your head, you just might have to announce your own resurrection.. You have to tell what and who is trying to take you down, "Go Ahead. Tear me down, I'll Be Back." "Cast me out, I'll Be Back." "Throw me away, I'll be Back." You have to announce your own comeback.

And don't worry if you haven't been down yet, just keep on living, everybody has a down day. But before you get to the downs, announce your come back and make good on your promise.

Romans 4:17, "speak those things that are not as though they were." You have to declare Psalms 118:17, "I will not die, but live, and declare the works of the Lord." Announce your own resurrection. And that you didn't find out in the streets, you found this out from the grave of somebody, who went down, but early Sunday morning, He got back up and so will you. Tell it, I'll be back.

> *He Got Back Up And So Will You.*

Not only will you be back but the breaking news from the Graveyard of the crucified savior tells us "Sometimes you can't stay where people left you."

The Angel said "He is not here, For he is risen as he said." Let me prove it to ya. "Come in and see where his body was lying. . . ."

And right there, Jesus might be trying to tell us that sometimes you can't stay where people left you."

Now listen here, the people who laid him there, did so with Good intentions. They were not malice as some folk are, but they laid him there so that he could receive a proper burial according to Jewish custom.

But if where people left you is not where you are supposed to be. You just might want to get up from there and get to where you belong. Jesus knew that he was not supposed to be surrounded by the dead, because he came so that we might have life and have it more abundantly. Jesus knew that he was not to stay in a cemetery, because he knew he was the Resurrection and the Life. And sometimes when you know that what God has for you is not where you are right now and where they left you. You just might have to get up and get to where you belong. Yes, they left you with three children to raise by yourself. Don't Stay There. Get up and get to where you belong. Yes, they left you to deal with debt you didn't create and issues in your body you didn't ask for, I understand, But Get up and Get to where you belong. Yes, they left you to go after another dog. To go after another company, to go after another temporary pleasure. But where they left you is not where you have to stay. And that is Good News from the Grave. They came looking for him, where he was. They came looking for him where they left him.

> ## Don't Stay There. Get Up And Get To Where You Belong.

And the people who left you in a certain place, in a certain mood, in a certain condition, will come back expecting to find you exactly where they left you. But you just might have to get up and get out and get to where you belong. Don't you let them come back and find you in the same situation they left you. Don't you let them come back and find you with the same mindset they left you with. Don't you let them come back and find you in the same seat, they left you with. Don't you let them come back and find you with the same level of faith they left you with. Don't you let them come back and find you with the same paint on the walls and furniture in your house.

Get Up and do something with what you have left. You owe it to yourself to MOVE ON. You owe it to yourself to not let them see you still mad. Still broke. Still crying. Still, hurting. Still insecure.

Get up and Get to where you belong and that's Good News from the Grave. Even God doesn't want his people in the same place where he left them. He wants them to go on to something greater. He said to his disciples, Greater works than these will ye do. Don't you let me come back and find you doing just what I did. But you ought to be doing more than what I did. And that's the breaking news from the grave.

Ephesians 1:13-14, tells us we must go from faith to faith and glory to glory.

You owe it to yourself to not get stuck, just coming to church, for Christmas, Mothers Day, New Years and Easter. Get up and Get to where you belong.

You owe it to yourself to not just come to church. But get up, come down the aisle, give your life to Christ, for real this time. But don't stop there. Live the life, He has called you to live. Get up and Get to where you belong.

Don't play with yourself in life. Time is winding down, it's time to get right with God and do HIS WORKS. Don't you let them come back and find you in the same situation they left you. They left you playing church. They left you tossed between two opinions. They left you and when they get back they will be looking for you to be doing what they left you doing. But I dare you CHANGE IT UP.

Jesus is trying to tell us that sometimes you can't stay where people left you."

And lastly, this detailed account, reported live by Matthew, shares with us: The Angel now tells the women, "And now, go quickly and tell his disciples… that he is going to Galilee, to meet them there." He is going to Galilee to meet them there. He did not say to meet them in Galilee. He said, Jesus is going to Galilee, to meet them there.

Jesus is saying, don't meet me there, BEAT ME THERE. And that's good news from the grave: Sometimes you have to point people to the place where God is going to show up.

The task of the women was to get the disciples there, before Jesus Got there. They were to get the disciples to the place where God is going to show up.

And it's time for us to stop pointing people to where he was, but point them to where He will show up. You have to stay in tune to who God is, so that when people come to you for the solution, you can point them to where God is going to show up.

Lets take for instance praise, the Bible says, "that God inhabits the praises of his people." That means anytime you praise God, he will show up. You don't wait until you see Him in the room, you praise Him, know that He is on the way. And watch Him show up. Don't meet him there, BEAT Him There.

Let's take prayer for example, the Bible says, "where two or three of you are gathered together in my name," he said, "I WILL BE in the midst." That means if you pray with somebody else in the name of Jesus, He will show up. Don't meet him there, BEAT Him There..

And that's Good News from the Grave. Sometimes you have to point people to where God is going to show.

Stop sending people to dead churches, send them where God is going to show up. Stop sending people into dead relationships, send them to places where God is going to show up.

Meet Him in Galilee! Umm Galilee. A two fold directive is given here.

One for the disciples and one for us. Galilee was the hometown of Jesus and his disciples. So Jesus tells the boys to meet me back at home. But for us. Galilee is interpreted as a circle or origin. Jesus is saying to us, "Meet Me Back Where We Started." And where we started was in a place where we walked in relationship with God. Where we talked with God. And Where we knew that We were God's Own.

But in order to meet Him again, you cannot go back, you can only go forward. And the only way to go forward is to Announce your own resurrections. And the only way to God forward is to refuse to stay where people left you, but get up and get to where you belong. And the only way to move forward is to point somebody else to where God is going to show up.

And the story says, the ladies are scared and excited at the same time. And on their way to tell somebody else to meet Jesus, they mess around and meet Him for themselves.

And that's good news for you. Maybe as you are on the way, to tell somebody else the Good News, the Good News just might meet you on your way.

> *Maybe as you are on the way, to tell somebody else the Good News, the Good News just might meet you on your way.*

Let me prove it to you.

Cathy is an average woman who works in a bakery in Wichita, Kansas, and has two rods in her hip. Cathy was saving up some money to buy her a new car and saved a little over 5000. One day as Catherine's boss was checking up on Cathy to see how the savings plan was going, Cathy revealed to her (Debbie), that she gave the money she was saving for the much needed car to a widow who was experiencing great financial distress.

Cathy's boss Debbie, was not surprised, but did not let it go. Debbie got out in the community and started raising money and developed a partnership with a local car dealer, and got a car for Cathy, because of what Cathy did for someone else. Sometimes as you are on the way to help somebody else, THE WAY Steps in and helps you.

Tell them to meet me in Galilee. And that's Good News from the grave… What are people spreading about you around town? When you are in over your head, when you are outnumbered and under-resourced?

You sometimes have to announce your own comeback.

You sometimes have to not stay where they left you.

You sometimes have to point people to the place where God is going to show up

And sometimes what you have been sent to tell somebody else, just might be the message you need, for yourself.

Good News from the Grave.

-NINE-

Peter raises a female disciple named Tabitha from the dead

Acts 9:36-42 (KJV)

36 Now there was at Joppa a certain disciple named Tabitha, which by interpretation is called Dorcas: this woman was full of good works and almsdeeds which she did.

37 And it came to pass in those days, that she was sick, and died: whom when they had washed, they laid her in an upper chamber.

38 And forasmuch as Lydda was nigh to Joppa, and the disciples had heard that Peter was there, they sent unto him two men, desiring him that he would not delay to come to them.

39 Then Peter arose and went with them. When he was come, they brought him into the upper chamber: and all the widows stood by him weeping, and shewing the coats and garments which Dorcas made, while she was with them.

40 But Peter put them all forth, and kneeled down, and prayed; and turning him to the body said, Tabitha, arise. And she opened her eyes: and when she saw Peter, she sat up.

41 And he gave her his hand, and lifted her up, and when he had called the saints and widows, presented her alive.

42 And it was known throughout all Joppa; and many believed in the Lord.

No Good Deed Goes Unpunished   Rev. John H. Gamble Jr.

Peter and Tabitha (also known as Dorcas)

Acts 9:36-42

About 10 or so years ago, China enlisted armies of ducks to prevent a plague of locusts that was engulfing valuable cropland. The Manasi locust station in northwest China would unleash 4,000 hungry ducks into surrounding fields to munch their way through as many of the insects as they can.

When asked about this strategy, one of the respondents said, "Ducks are the best way to get rid of locusts because they have such a big appetite." But listen to the next part! He said, "After two or three months, they typically weigh around two kilos and can be sold to markets and roast duck restaurants." They used the ducks to save their crops, but then rather than allowing the ducks to live free, they capture them, and sell them to restaurants to be eaten wrapped in thin pancakes with plum sauce and spring onions.

Hence, the title of this sermon: No Good Deed Goes Unpunished. It's an age old saying that holds to the principle that it is not worth doing good, because things we do that are beneficial to othersoften go unappreciated. Sometimes they are met with hostility or resentment. On the other hand, those who might appreciate it, then come back with a laundry lists of additional requests.

In other words, it is hard to do good when you feel like what you do will not be appreciated. It's hard to do good when you feel like those who do good end up worse of then those who do evil. It's the classic complaint of Jeremiah when he went to God, with the question, "Why does the ways of the wicked prosper? Why does it seem like those who deal in treachery end up doing well?"

And that's the question that undergirds this text, because in the text, Luke the writer of Acts introduces us to a situation where it seems like the person who did everything right dies. The Bible says,

> *36 At Joppa there was a certain disciple named Tabitha, which is translated Dorcas. This woman was full of good works and charitable deeds which she did. 37 But it happened in those days that she became sick and died. When they had washed her, they laid her in an upper room.*

Here is this woman, Tabitha, who seems to be doing everything right. The Bible says that she is full of good works. One translation says she was always doing kind things for others. Here is a woman who was never thinking about herself. She spent her time looking out for others and helping the poor. This woman was doing for people what others were not willing to do, and the Bible says that she becomes sick and dies.

And isn't it amazing that the people who seem to do the least often live the longest? Isn't it interesting that people who don't want to be about anything can still survive, and yet it seems like those who try to do the right things, and be on point often get the short end of the stick? It's the people who work the hardest and try their best that often end up sick, underappreciated, and used up. It's sad, but it's true, when people know that you have a lot to offer, and when people know you have a lot to give, they will continue to take and take from you, without depositing into you and before you know it, you are tapped out and they are trying to figure out who they can get to fill the void you have now left in their lives.

You don't believe me. Here are some of the most thankless jobs in America. Customer service representatives (deal with people's attitude),

Sanitation workers/garbage collectors (dangerous, dirty work), government employees (have to work under the reminder that my taxes pay your salary), administrative assistants (have to deal with difficult bosses and difficult people), food service workers like waiters/busboys (deal with no tips/tips like "try Jesus"). What about the teacher or the window cleaner? You get my point! Jobs that require service and serving others are often the most thankless jobs. People expect you to do it and they are not necessarily grateful for it.

Sometimes we have to be careful not to allow people to use us until we are used up. That's even implicit in the text. I don't believe it is coincidence that this woman is named Tabitha, or Dorcas, in the text. That name translates to be gazelle. And if you don't know what a gazelle is, a gazelle is like a deer or an antelope. It is a graceful, beautiful animal that lives in the wild. It's swift in that has bursts of speed up to 60 miles per hour. But they often fall prey to leopards and other big cats not because they can become so focused on the grass they are eating, or the view they see in front of them, that they forget to check on their own safety. They forget to observe what's around them and, as a result, they fall victim to the attack.

And the truth of the matter is that serving God can almost put you in similar situations. Serving God can put you in situations where it seems like you are vulnerable for attack. Don't fool yourself, the more you serve the Lord, the more likely it is that people will criticize you and analyze what you are doing. People will find more fault in you the more you do for the Lord! You will work yourself to the ground, and people will help you bury yourself when they stand to benefit from it. I'm in the text. The Bible says,

This woman was full of good works and charitable deeds which she did. 37 But it happened in those days that she became sick and died. When they had washed her, they laid her in an upper room.

Notice the text says, "In those days" which means that Tabitha/Dorcas didn't die suddenly. She was sick for a while. And my question is where are all of the people she helped now that she is sick? She was full of good works, but now that she can't do for herself, are those same people who she helped, there to help her? The answer is not quite explicit in the text, but notice, we don't see anyone do anything for her until she dies. We don't see a doctor in the text. We don't see them trying to care for her in the text. She is working. She gets sick. And when she dies, they prepare her for burial.

It seems like she has worked for everyone else, but who is working for her? Let me suggest that this text is for the unsung heroes. This text is for those who do for people, help people, look out for people, and they don't get much recognition for it. And here is the message of the text. God sees what we do for him it is God who rewards our faithfulness. Notice that Dorcas was referred to as a disciple. She was a follower of Christ. She did not walk with Christ, like Mary and Martha. She doesn't have the military pedigree of a Deborah. She doesn't have the love story of a Ruth. But she was a disciple of the Lord. Because of what she did for God, God made sure that her sickness was not her end. God made sure that her condition was not critical. God sent Peter to Joppa, so that we might see that when you do what God has called you to do, your good deeds of faith, are not a source of stress, but they are in fact a connector to the blessing that God has in store for your life. The Bible says that Dorcas became sick and died.

38 And since Lydda was near Joppa, and the disciples had heard that Peter was there, they sent two men to him, imploring him not to delay in coming to them. 39 Then Peter arose and went with them.

Now Lydda and Joppa were about 35 miles apart. But because Dorcas was such a good person and see did so much good, it is reasonable to believe that Peter and others knew who she was, which was why Peter would get up immediately and go. And we know by the end of the story, Dorcas is alive and because she gets up many believe on the Lord.

But here is the lesson. You can do good deeds. You can be a good person. But when people can see how God has changed your life, that's where faith comes in. The transformation of lives does not come from what we do for people; but it comes from what people see God do in us.

And this leads me to my first point. Because in order for people to change, they have to see the change in you, which means they have to see you for who you are, more than what you have. And this is implicit in the text. The Bible says,

39 Then Peter arose and went with them. When he had come, they brought him to the upper room. And all the widows stood by him weeping, showing the tunics and garments which Dorcas had made while she was with them. 40 But Peter put them all out, and knelt down and prayed. And turning to the body he said, "Tabitha, arise." And she opened her eyes, and when she saw Peter she sat up.

Now, let's just deal with the first part. He comes into the house. They bring him to where she is. The widows are crying. Now these are not the hired mourners, who get paid to make noise. These are not the people who make money off somebody else's misfortune, but these widows are mourning because they know their lives will not be same without her, not because of who she is, but because of what she give them. She sowed

202

their clothes. She made what they were wearing, and perhaps they were now wondering, who was going to help them survive. I mean, this text is the text that is used to support women as deacons and ministers, because it was an issue with the widows that created the office of deacons in the first place. Here we see a woman, Dorcas, who is doing the work and the people (the widows), are wondering who is going to do the work now. But he Bible says, Peter puts them all out of the room, and it's not because they are bad people, it's because they have the wrong focus.

And when God seeks to change our lives, and when God chooses to bless our lives, it's not as simple as him paying us for what we have done, because the truth is that we could never repay him for what he did. The Cross is an un-payable debt. But Jesus changes our lives not because of what we do, but because of who we are.

- John says, "He came unto his own and his own received him not.... Become the sons of God"

Our salvation is not of works, but by faith

- Paul says (in Ephesians), "For it is by grace you have been saved, through faith--and this is not from yourselves, it is the gift of God. Not of works, lest any man would be able to boast."

Peter wants the people to understand that this resurrection is not a result of her works; it is a result of faith. That's what we believe as Christians. We don't get to heaven because we did a lot of good deeds... nice person... smiled at everybody... We get to heaven because of our faith in Jesus Christ.

- 1 Corinthians 15, Paul says, it is preached that Christ has been raised from the dead, how can some of you say that there is no resurrection of the dead?_17 And if Christ has not been raised, your faith is futile; you are still in your sins.18 Then those also who have fallen asleep in Christ are lost.... (HE SAYS) But someone may ask, "How are the dead raised? With what kind of body will they come?" 51 Listen, I tell you a mystery: We will not all sleep, but we will all be changed-- 52 in a flash, in the twinkling of an eye, at the last trumpet. For the trumpet will sound, the dead will be raised imperishable, and we will be changed. 53 For the perishable must clothe itself with the imperishable, and the mortal with immortality.

I don't know about anyone else, but I thank God that it is not what I do, that gets me into heaven. Because if truth be told, there are some things I do that look more HELLISH than they do HEAVENLY! (And I am not by myself!.... There are some place you go that are not too heavenly.... Things you say/do..... Tell your neighbor, "Don't judge me. Pray for me.")

They have to see you for who you are, more than what you have. But then they have to see that Prayer Changes things. The Bible says,

40 But Peter put them all out, and knelt down and prayed. And turning to the body he said, "Tabitha, arise." And she opened her eyes, and when she saw Peter she sat up.

And I know that this is a simple point. I know that it is not that deep. But sometimes you don't have to be deep, when the Bible says it clearly. Peter sees the woman dead, and he prays. It's no different than what Jesus did at the tomb of Lazarus, when they rolled away the stone, he prayed. It's no different than what Elijah did when the widow's son died> He cried unto the Lord in prayer.

Sometimes you have to go before the Lord in prayer. The Bible says that he knelt down. He took the posture of humility. He understood that the only way that this woman was going to live again was if the Lord stepped in. And that what prayer can be in your life. Prayer can be the invitation for the Lord to step into the situation, knowing that when God steps in, the situation immediately turns in your favor. You know one of my favorite stories in scripture; I talk about it at least once every six or seven sermons. Jehoshaphat and the army of Judah against the army of the people of Mount Seir (the Edomites), Ammonites, and the Moabites. He led the people in fasting and prayer. And my favorite line of the prayer: 2 Chronicles 20:12, Jehoshaphat tells the Lord, "For we have no might against this great company that cometh against us; we don't know what to do: but our eyes are upon you"

The response was, "17 You won't need to fight in this battle: set yourselves, stand still, and see the salvation of the LORD with you, O Judah and Jerusalem: fear not, nor be dismayed; tomorrow go out against them: for the LORD will be with you."

That's why Peter prayed, because prayer is a reminder to the people that the Lord is with you. And I don't about anyone but it's not always in my praise that I am reminded of God's presence. It's not always in my preaching that I am reminded of His presence. But it is when I pray, that I am reminded that God is on my side.

Prayer is The Power of Attorney. He says the Power of attorney is the legal right to sign on someone else's behalf. That's exactly what happens when you pray. He says when Christians pray to the Father, the Holy Ghost delivers our prayer to the Father. But before, God responds, he looks over to Jesus and asks Him if He is signing the note. Jesus is our power of attorney. He is the one who signs off on our prayers. He is the one who gives us access to God.

And prayer changes things, because it gives us access to the only One who can make change and that is the Lord. And I know there is somebody who can testify that I talked to Lord. I prayed about it. And God changed it. God worked it out.

Well are there some prayer warriors in the house? Are there some people who believe in the power of prayer!

Peter knows about the Power of Prayer in Acts 9, because of what He experienced in Acts 4 – Peter and John locked up for preaching Christ. They were released the next day, warned not to preach in His name again, but they could not be beaten because the people were praising God in the streets because the man at the gate called beautiful had been changed. He was in the temple walking leaping and praising God. But the Bible says that when the people heard about what Peter and John has been through, they prayed… When they had finished praying, the place where they were gathered was shaken. They were all filled with the Holy Spirit. It was easy for everyone to speak the Word of God.

Prayer changes things!

I am done. They had to see her for who she was more than what she had. They had to understand that prayer changes things. But finally, they needed to see that everyone needs to be lifted up sometime. The Bible says,

> *41 Then he gave her his hand and lifted her up; and when he had called the saints and widows, he presented her alive.*

Now notice, even in the first part of the resurrection, Peter called her name, she opened her eyes and she sat up. But this next verse shows us that while, she sat up, she couldn't get up until Peter lifted her up. In other words, Dorcas was used to everything on her own. She was used to being the one who did for everyone else. But this showed her that there are times when even the helpers need help. There are times when we all get weak. We all get tired. We all get weary. And we need some help. The Bible says that Peter gave her his hand. Now if she would have let her pride settle in, she could have refused his hand. She would have been alive, but stuck in the bed. But because she took the assistance, she was able to get out of the bed, because she could not only rely on her strength, but she could rely in Peter's strength.

And that's where I want to close this sermon. We may be strong. We may be tough. We may be independent.... Survivor. But we all can get tired sometimes. We all can use somebody to help us from being stuck where we are.

And the good news is that God has provided a Peter in our life to help lift us up.

I mean, even Jesus got some assistance carrying the cross. He was assisted by Simon of Cyrene.

We all can use somebody! So, who are you willing to help? Who is willing to help you?

A Reason To Live   Dr. Willie J. Thompson Jr.

Acts 9:36-42 (CEV)

36 In Joppa there was a follower named Tabitha. Her Greek name was Dorcas, which means "deer." She was always doing good things for people and had given much to the poor. 37 But she got sick and died, and her body was washed and placed in an upstairs room. 38 Joppa wasn't far from Lydda, and the followers heard that Peter was there. They sent two men to say to him, "Please come with us as quickly as you can!" 39 Right away, Peter went with them. The men took Peter upstairs into the room. Many widows were there crying. They showed him the coats and clothes that Dorcas had made while she was still alive. 40 After Peter had sent everyone out of the room, he knelt down and prayed. Then he turned to the body of Dorcas and said, "Tabitha, get up!" The woman opened her eyes, and when she saw Peter, she sat up. 41 He took her by the hand and helped her to her feet. Peter called in the widows and the other followers and showed them that Dorcas had been raised from death. 42 Everyone in Joppa heard what had happened, and many of them put their faith in the Lord.

The book of Acts, authored by Luke a Greek physician is a document of primary historical value both for the history of the church and the ancient world. Apart from Acts the gap between the Gospels or Good News of Jesus Christ and the Epistles, or letters written by the apostles and others would be almost unbridgeable, for there would be no explanation available for the transition from the ministry of Jesus to the doctrine and evangelism of the church.

If that be the case then we can agree that Acts has two distinct purposes, one to be a bridge between two time periods and the other to provide explanation or give us the reason why we do what we do. If then a bridge, Acts becomes a structure built to span physical obstacles such as a body of water, valley or road, for the purpose of providing passage over the obstacle. So in the natural, even as in the spirit, when we open the text of Acts, we open opportunities to one encounter a structure, a power and unction that is constructed in the span of the obstacle you are facing, with the sole purpose of providing passage over the obstacle. It encourages us, because there are some things that you will not have to go through, because something is gonna happen, something is going to arise, and come together that will provide you safe passage over the obstacle, instead of going through it. Acts is a bridge, built the span of the obstacle, meaning it is as long as the problem is. And its sole purpose is to get you over to the other, un stayed, unharmed and un affected by what you had to pass over.

But not only a bridge, but Acts serves a second purpose of providing an explanation of how we got from the ministry of Jesus to the doctrine and outreach or evangelism of the church. It gives us the why behind what we do, or more exact the reason. So many people do things because they see them but not always know why they do what is being done.

A young woman used to watch her mother cook during the holiday season, and saw her mother always cut a significant portion off of the end of a ham. And when she grew older she did what she saw, not totally understanding why her mother cut the ham. She later found out that the mother cut a significant portion off not because something was wrong with the ham part, but did it because the pot she had was not big enough to accommodate the ham that she was given so she cut it, to make it fit.

And when we encounter the book of Acts we are given the reason or explanation of how the church began to do what it does, during the time of transition.

There was a time when children would never ask an adult why, but in this generation we've encountered a group of people who need to not just understand what, but they want to know why. And Because I said so, it's not the answer any longer.

And not knowing the reason, will cause your understanding to be off. Just Ask Earth, Wind in Fire, in their song reasons, who went in for one reason, and ended up getting caught up for another reason. Reason being here, because the love won't disappear.

Understanding the reason why will help you make better choices about what is going on in your life right now. Just ask another set of brothers, known as Dru Hill, who were having a hard time with a sister they were always there for, she started spending less and less time with the brother and wanted to hang out with her friends more than her man, and came out with a song on its 1998 album a song entitled "Give Me One Good Reason." "Why should I stay, your love is out of season, be on your way."

> "Why should I stay, your love is out of season, be on your way."

Knowing the reason will reveal things to you, that you took for granted or that you never paid attention to before. Just ask Betty Wright, who in her 1972 song describes a "Clean Up Woman" and Betty says, "A clean up woman is a woman, who gets all the love, we girls leave behind. The reason I know so much about her is because she picked up a man of mine." You ought to take some time to understand the reason behind what's going on in your life.

Acts explains to us how the church picked up where Jesus left off.

Listen in:

What's the reason behind our unity, because when we all get on one accord, the Spirit of God can flow through us (Acts 2).

What's the reason behind our giving, because we give to prove that all we have belongs to God and one another (Acts 4).

What's the reason behind our worship? Because when we worship we provide opportunity for God's people to meet with God and each other (Acts 5)

What's the reason behind our obedience? Because if what we do is of GOD, God will fight for us and we rather obey God than man (Acts 5).

What's the reason behind our trust in God's Word? Because we know grass withers, flowers fade, but the word of God will stand for ever.

What is the reason behind the need for the Holy Ghost? Because the Holy Ghost will give you power to stand like Stephen and speak truth to power.

What's the reason behind our Baptism? Because our baptism is so simple, so that people like the Ethiopian Eunuch can find a puddle of water and be baptized after hearing the word of the Lord.

Why did God blind Saul? So God could finally give him sight. Why are people sick? Sometimes, so God can show up and provide healing. Why are people in trouble, so we walk with them until they get out. Why is the world so dark and crazy? So you can show up and become the light of the World.

Here is Acts the church is crossing safely over with some understanding of their plight. But the Message translation opens this text with some keywords that I need to extract, and it says "Down the road a way in Joppa." Understanding the reason, will not just help you in your giving, your believing, your unity and your understanding, when you are on the top or just right now, but it will also guide you, Down the road."

And the Bible says, "down the road in Joppa, there was a disciple named Tabitha. She was well known for doing good works and helping out. And during the time when Peter was in the area she became sick and died. Her friends prepared her body for burial and put it in a cool room.

I would like to suggest this bridge of a text and the explanation of a transition may give us a Reason to Live.

Tabitha, a good woman. Tabitha, whose name means gazelle. Tabitha, who did good works. Tabitha, who helped many people. Tabitha, who got sick. Tabitha, who eventually dies as a result of her sickness. Tabitha who was a disciple and follower of Christ. Tabitha, a good person. Tabitha, a believer dies and is revived, but let's look to see if her story gives us a few reasons to live.

Tabitha's story may tell us, you need to live: "To see that the people you have been a friend to, when given the opportunity, will be a friend to you."

The text records in verses 36-39, "Tabitha was always doing good things for people, and had given much to the poor. But when she got sick and died, the followers, the other disciples, went and found Peter to come and see about her."

That's a really good reason to live. Just to see that the people you have been a friend to, when given the opportunity, will be a friend back to

212

you. Everyday you want to live so that the good works you extend, when needed, will one day be extended back to you. Tabitha lived a life of sowing and a life of blessing. The text does not say what exactly she did at this point, but it does share with us that what she was doing was good. Have you ever met somebody that is always taking and not giving? Have you ever met someone that is always extracting and never depositing? Seriously, taking attention, and never giving attention, asking for stuff and never giving stuff to anybody? Or maybe you met some people who just give to people so that they can one day get in return?

Tabitha needed to revive so that she could see that one day the people you have been a friend to, when given the opportunity, will be a friend back to you. When she died, they did not just let her good works go unnoticed, they did not just let death have the final say. When she died, they washed her, cleaned her up and took her to an upper room and when they heard Peter was near, they ran to get him to come and see about her. One day the same things you have done for others, others will rise up and do for you. And when you have been a friend to others, don't worry about the back stabbers, the haters and the people who used you, because the people that were really your friends, will pick you up from your place of death, wash you off, and run and get you some help. Now according to Jake from Scandal, yes some bad things happen to good people." But according to Galatians 6:7; "Do not be deceived God is not mocked, whatsoever a man or woman sows, that so shall he also reap." So if you sow good , good will come back to you. If you sow love, love will come back to you, If you sow much, much will

> *One day the people you have been a friend to, when given the opportunity, will be a friend back to you.*

come back to you. And didn't you read Proverbs, 18:24, that says "to obtain friends, you must first be friendly." You have a reason to live, even if it is just to see that the people you have been a friend to, when given the opportunity, will be a friend to you.

She dies, she is washed and taken up stairs and placed in an upper room, laid out nicely. Companions of hers, go and get pastor Peter to come and see about her. And when Peter arrives, the room is packed. They are having a jam packed viewing, and the bibles records "Many widows were there crying. They showed him the many coats and clothes that Dorcas had made while she was still alive."

And there it is right there, another reason to live. Might this story and record of Tabitha, life and death give us another reason to live, and that is: "To see the impact of your works in the broader world and society."

So many times we limit our good works to inner sanctuary servitude. This sister was not praised because she sang in the choir, she was not praised because she led all the prayer services. She was not praised because she wore the finest clothes to church. She never had on a mini skirt, she always wore a nice hat. She was not praised because she knew to honor and greet and treat inside the walls of the church. This sister was not honored because she was on every committee or ministry. She was a disciple, but she had a broader impact on not just her church, but in the streets and in the marketplace. She was a woman who knew how to work with her hands and used her gifts from God to not just bless people in the house, she didn't mind blessing people in the streets.

When Peter arrives, they don't show her name in the worship guide, they show him that when it was cold, she made coats. They showed him that when people were naked, she made clothes for their backs. I want to argue, because she didn't mind being a blessing, she provoked a blessing on her business, and her business was so well, that from her access she was able to be a blessing to the world and the broader society.

Now sister, I know we call you sister up in here, but what do they call you in the streets? What do they call you in the marketplace? What do they call you in the broader society? They did not say much to Peter, but what they did say tells us that she did more than just be a disciple. And its time for the believers and disciples of Christ, to not just want in-house impact, but it's time to get in the marketplace, and do good works. It's time to own hospitals and do good works. It's time to launch a clothing line and do good work. It's time to open your own salon and boutique and do good works. We love you up in here, but it's time for followers and disciples to expand their reach. To stretch their impact and influence to the utter most parts of business and society.

Oh you a woman? So what? Didn't you read, Proverbs 31? "She is like the merchant ships, She considers a field and buys it; She sees that her trading is profitable." She was about that business. She didn't just want in-house impact, she wanted to reach the unreachable and touch the untouchable. She did not just clap her hands, she went out and did like Fat Joe and Lil Wayne said, "Make it Rain." Oprah should not be the only one, building schools in African countries, so should you. Joyce Meyer should be the only one to return to her community and build a state of the art DREAM CENTER, so should you. Toni Morrison, can't be the only accomplished writer and author, what about you? Marissa Meyer, at 38 cant be the only CEO of YAHOO, what about you? Ellen Degeneres can't be the only female comedian and show host, so should you? Condoleezza Rice, can't be the only one to get a Ph.D. in Political Science and become Secretary of State, What about you? Hillary Rodham Clinton and Shirley Chisolm, can't be the only female presidential hopeful, so should you. And Olivia Pope can't be the only gladiator, what about you? We, like Tabitha, can't limit ourselves to in-house servitude, we need to revive to see the impact of our works in the world and broader society.

Pastor Peter, look what she has done for us and left for us and gave to us. And it was good. She left something with them they had to talk about. But guess what, she was still dead? She had made her transition, she was in the place of preparation for burial. It looked like all hope was lost. She was at the most critical point in her life and the final judgment was death. And from our view, you can't go any lower than death. When you die, it is over. Death is the one thing you can't come back from. You can be healed of a sickness. You can be healed of a divorce. You can't be delivered from an addiction. But where do you run from death?

The Bible says Peter put everyone out of the room, and prayed. He heard what she had done for friends and saw what friends would do for her. He saw that her influence as a believer went far beyond the four walls of the temple and reached out into the world and the larger society. But even after all that he prayed to God. And the bible says he turned to the body and said, "Tabitha, Get Up!" The woman opened her eyes, she saw Peter and sat up. He took her by the hand and helped her to her feet. The story records Peter called in the widows and the followers and showed them that Dorcas had been raised from the dead. And everyone in (Clairton), Joppa, heard what had happened and many of them put their faith in the Lord.``

Lastly, this story of this woman's life and death gives us one more reason to live. So she tells us you need to revive: "To see that the challenging events in your life, when conquered, will cause others to believe in Christ."

> *"To see that the challenging events in your life, when conquered, will cause others to believe in Christ."*

So many times we don't want to go through challenging times in our life. So many times we don't want the embarrassment of a sickness, a divorce, and a failure. We don't want the bottom to fall out and we don't want our homes to be set on fire. We spend some much time trying to avoid problems and do everything right just so we can fit in and never stick out. We try to hide it and keep it on the hush. We try to act strong even when we are weak and falling apart. We don't want to have to fight, because when we fight we come out with scars. We don't want to have to start over, because we have to live with the memory of where we were. We don't want to try again because the last attempt did not work. But don't you know that the thing you are going through just might be the thing that is going to cause someone else to believe. This sister was a good person, who had experienced a very bad thing, but when the situation had been conquered, other people started believing in Christ. And that's a reason to live. They need to see, "that many are the afflictions of the righteous, but the Lord will bring them out of them all." They need to see: "He knows the way that I take, and after I've been tried in the fire, you shall come forth as pure gold." They need to see that: "After you have suffered for a little while, the God of all grace will restore you, and make you strong, firm and steadfast." They need to see: "That the sufferings of this present time are not worthy to be compared to the glory which shall be revealed in us." And that's a reason to live.

May I suggest that your challenge may be the channel of someone else's change. When she was revived, everybody heard about it and many people believed in the Lord. So go on through, because it's gonna help somebody else come to know Christ. Go on through, it's going to help someone else learn to lean and depend on Jesus. So go on through, conquer that thing, win that battle, stronghold that struggle. Because when you come out, its going to make somebody else say "I have decided to follow Jesus." And that's a reason to live. Somebody's watching your challenge. Somebody's watching your storm. Somebody is watching your struggle. Trying to see if you curse God and die, or take courage and live. They are trying to see if you are going to break, or bend your knees and cry out to your father. They are trying to see if you are going to give up, or give in to the will of your Father God. And when you get up. And you will get up. The same folk that mourn your loss will celebrate your victory and even more people will come to know Christ because of your life.

A writer once said,

> "the greatest sermons are not recorded in scripture, they are found in the everyday lives of people who dare to trust God, and see Him deliver."

It's Revival, WHY? Because You Have A Reason To Live.

-TEN-

Paul raises Eutychus from the dead

Acts 20:9-12 (KJV)

9 And there sat in a window a certain young man named Eutychus, being fallen into a deep sleep: and as Paul was long preaching, he sunk down with sleep, and fell down from the third loft, and was taken up dead.

10 And Paul went down, and fell on him, and embracing him said, Trouble not yourselves; for his life is in him.

11 When he therefore was come up again, and had broken bread, and eaten, and talked a long while, even till break of day, so he departed.

12 And they brought the young man alive, and were not a little comforted.

There's Still Life In Me!   Rev. John H. Gamble Jr.

Paul and Eutychus

Acts 20

It was a Good Morning America feature. Rob Elliott, a 45 year old attorney ran a 7.5-mile race a week before the sudden cardiac arrest, and 3 miles that morning. He would have never have suspected that he would be a candidate for this type of problem. But on this particular morning, a day before their 14th anniversary, Rob Elliot told his wife Dana that he was unable to move a muscle and then blacked out. As Elliot went into cardiac arrest, Dana called 911, performed CPR and searched for his pulse, but couldn't find one.

When the paramedics arrived at the Elliotts' home, they continued the work his wife had started, even though they said they couldn't find his pulse either. Rob Elliott was even hooked up to a cardiac monitor, which showed no pulse. For nearly 30 minutes, they were continuously checking his pulse, and then finally, a pulse, and unbelievable miracle was taking place.

Not that Cardiac arrest is irreversible. If it's treated within a few minutes with an electric shock, the heart can be restored to a normal heartbeat. However, a person's chances of survival are reduced by 7 percent to 10 percent with every minute that passes without defibrillation. Under any circumstances, most people who survive get their pulse back in the first five or 10 minutes, and usually there is some no damage to the brain.

When Elliott's wife, Dana, arrived at the hospital with their two young children the day after his cardiac arrest, she expected to find her husband clinging to life. Instead she found him conscious and smiling. He was sitting up, and he greeted her saying, "Hi, babe."

One month after the near death experience, Elliot again feels to like a picture of health saying he feels no different than he did before the frightening incident.

Elliot was saved because his wife kept working on him, performing CPR even when there was no pulse. The message for GMA audience was that everyone needs to learn CPR, because this man was not dead; there was still life in him. It was faint, it couldn't be detected. Even the most advanced machines to which he was connected could read his pulse, but the life in this man was still there.

And I think that the message of the story is the message of the text. Because I believe that any story in the Bible has spiritual significance. And in this text, we come across a young man named Eutychus who falls from a third story window, and is presumed dead, until Paul leaves where he is, goes to where the boy is, and touches him while making the statement, "There's still life in him."

And I just believe that part of the problem that many people face is that we are often set up to fall. We are born with potential, born with possibilities but circumstances and situations in our lives are set up in such a way to make it easier for us to fall than to stand tall. In the text we see this, because the Bible says,

> *9 And in a window sat a certain young man named Eutychus, who was sinking into a deep sleep. He was overcome by sleep; and as Paul continued speaking, he fell down from the third story and was taken up dead.*

You don't even have to go beyond his name to realize what I am trying to say. The name Eutychus means "fortunate". And we know that when people named their children in the bible, the name reflected either the present condition under which the child was born, or a future prediction of who the child would become. So, by Eutychus being named fortunate, the implication could be that he was born into favorable circumstances, or he would grow into favorable circumstances. But in the text, this young man who is named as one who is fortunate ends up in an unfortunate situation. He is set up to fall. He is placed in a situation that would hurt him more than help him.

And this is the crazy part of the story. Eutychus is this fortunate young man, but he comes the church to die. Notice what happens in the text. The Bible says,

> 7 Now on the first day of the week, when the disciples came together to break bread, Paul, ready to depart the next day, spoke to them and continued his message until midnight.

In other words, this young falls to his death while he is in worship, which should be a warning to us all. Because you can come to church but you can still fall. You can come to church and not receive the message. You can come to church and not get what you need to make it to through the next week, or even the next day. This young man comes to church, to hear a word, and ends up in a worse situation than he was when he walked through the door. And we've got to be careful, children of God, because a Eutychus can come to church every Sunday. Every Sunday somebody can walk into this house of worship and they can be filled with potential, and whether they flourish or whether they fall can depend on how we treat them. How we respond to them could determine whether they go back out in the street. How we respond to them could determine that next hit. How we respond to them could determine if they go back into that abusive situation. We don't know who's coming through the doors. We don't know who's listening in. Maybe some of us are like Eutychus ourselves. Young, full of energy, big dreams and ideas. Strong and hopeful. And we have come to hear a word from the Lord. Don't kill the life that's in me. Don't set me up to fall. Don't set me up to fail.

And that's what we see in the text. Eutychus was set up to fail. First, because he was pushed aside to watch, rather than pulled in. It's in the text,

9 And in a window sat a certain young man named Eutychus.

That's the problem right there. Eutychus is in the window. Eutychus is in fellowship with the other believers. They are breaking bread, eating, and Paul is preaching. That means they are sitting at the table. Here's the question: If they are sitting at the table, why is Eutychus in the window? Here is my supposition. Eutychus is a boy. He is not of age yet. I preached this text before (4/26/14 reclamation breakfast) and Eutychus was not allowed into the gathering of men. He was curious about what Paul was saying, so in order to hear the message, he climbed three stories into a window, and sat where he would go unnoticed so that he could hear what Paul had to say. It is now bring deal now, but culturally, it was not appropriate for children to be in the room with adults. Some of you remember, especially if you grew up in the South, young folks were not supposed to be around grown folk conversation. As a matter of fact, if two adults were talking and you were nearby, you better pretend like you couldn't hear what they are talking about, and God help you if you make a comment, because you would end up with your teeth down your throat.

That makes sense for casual conversation, but when we are talking spiritual discipleship and the message of salvation, too many of us push people aside and get all of the Jesus for ourselves.

For Eutychus, it was his age, but that's not the only reason we push people aside. We push people aside for how they dress. We push people aside for how they smell. We push people aside for their choice of friends…. relationship preferences. And we fail to remember that if they if get here, they came here to get a Word, just like you and me. As a matter of fact, for some people, it's hard to come to worship. For some people, the guilt of their past, the reality of their present, and the dismal nature of their future, for them to come through the doors is like Eutychus climbing up the wall to the window. It's hard for them to come into to worship!

What are you saying, preacher? Somebody should have noticed Eutychus in the window and brought him closer to Paul. Maybe he doesn't fall asleep and fall out the window, if they act like they wanted him there. Maybe he doesn't almost die if he is allowed to participate and does not feel like he is pushed away. In other words, nobody should have to feel like they are on the outside looking in the house of God. Nobody should feel like they are sitting in the window when they come to worship. Everyone should feel like they belong in the house of God. Nobody knows what I went through this week. Nobody knows the stress I have to deal with in my life. Nobody knows the struggles I have had to endure, and how hard it is to keep a smile on my face. And so, when I come into the house of the Lord, somebody needs to make me feel like I belong. Somebody ought to be glad to see me. (That's why we have the greeting period, welcome! Not for a bathroom break. But so that somebody can show me that they are glad I made it!)

Come on somebody! Are you glad to be here? And I am sure you didn't want to be sitting here by yourself! I am excited when I get to church and I see the people of God. And I don't discriminate. I am as excited to see the left side of the church as I am to see the right side of the church. I am as excited to see the babies as I am to see the mothers. I am as excited to see the deacons as I am to see the trustees. (I am as excited.... CALL NAMES)

The Psalmist said, "I was glad when they said unto me, 'Let us go into the house of the Lord'."

Somebody ought to say, "I'm glad I'm here!" But then you need to look at your neighbor and say, "I'm glad you're here!"

Eutychus was set up to fall. First, because he was pushed aside to watch, rather than pulled in. But then, Eutychus was set up to fall, because Paul was preaching and not connecting.

> *9 And there sat in a window a certain young man named Eutychus, being fallen into a deep sleep: and as Paul was long preaching, he sunk down with sleep, and fell down from the third loft, and was taken up dead.*

The text says that Paul was LONG preaching. Now, verse 7 says that they came together for dinner. Dinner time in the text was similar to dinner time today. The Jews would offer the sacrifice from 3 pm to 5 pm. They would then take the lamb slain home and prepare it for dinner that night. So, if we assume that to be the standard, then we can say that dinner started anywhere between 7 PM to 9PM. At dinner, Paul begins to preach, and continues preaching until midnight. In other words, depending on the travel time from temple to home, and the time of preparation for the meal, Paul could have been preaching anywhere from 3 to 5 hours. Don't miss it. The focused attention span for the average human being is about 20 minutes, after which a person must choose to refocus. Here is Paul preaching at least 10 times longer than a person is capable of listening. Eutychus is in the window, and not at the table, and then we wonder why Eutychus falls out of the window.

There is nothing worse than preaching at people, and not connecting with people. Don't keep telling me what I doing wrong, if you don't want to help me get it right. Don't keep telling me what I need to fix, if you are not willing to fix it. Don't miss it. Here is Paul, probably preaching about discipleship and evangelism. He is probably charging the disciples to go out and bring people in. But yet, he is connecting with the one person who made the greatest effort to get there. We have to be careful to connect. Let me say this to those the preachers, Sunday School teachers, worship leaders, those of us who lead the people. If we can't connect, it doesn't matter what comes out of my mouth. I listen to the feedback on my preaching. I pay attention to what you as a congregation feel about the messages I give every week. Because there is no need to preach (and especially preach long), if it's not connecting to the people we are preaching to. We need the word to make a difference in our lives. We need the word of God to change us and help us. We need to be able to open the Word of God and be able to understand what's in it so we can live it and apply it.

Don't preach at me; connect with me. Bring it to my level. Make where I can understand it. I've had some people challenge me to be more eloquent. They suggest my pedigree and my education to push me to show my polish. They think that the use of my urban examples in my preaching and speaking is a disservice to my academic achievement. In other words, I sound too black. The only grade of "C" I received in grade school was in preaching! But I refused to change my style. I refused to change the content of my sermon because I don't just need to sound like a good preacher; I need my preaching needs to connect with the people I am preaching to. Obama has to give great speeches. Bill Clinton has to give great addresses. I'm a preacher, and I want to connect with the people. And if somebody doesn't get it in the message, I want them to text me. I want them to inbox me. I want to talk about it. Because my goal is not to sound the best, my goal is to change lives.

And let me turn the corner and tell you children of God, that's why the best preaching that can ever be done, doesn't take place in the pulpit. It takes place every day when you live outside of these four walls. When people see the hell that you go through, when people see how you struggle to pay your bills just like they do, when people see you stretch, stress, and strain just like they do, and yet you have praise on your lips. You have joy in your heart. That is what connects with the people. It's not long sermons. It's not the pontifications of those who feel they have arrived. Sometimes people just need you to walk up to them and say, "I'm praying for you." "I've been there just like you." "God is making a way for me, and He will do the same for you."

All of us have a word in us that can connect with others who need to hear about Christ. All of us have a testimony of what the Lord has done. Is there anybody here who can say, "When I look back over my life, and I think things over…."

Eutychus was set up to fall. First, because he was pushed aside to watch, rather than pulled in. Secondly, Paul was preaching and not connecting. But finally, Eutychus was set up to fall, because they drew the wrong conclusion. If you read the second part of verse 9, it says,

> He sunk down with sleep, and fell down from the third loft, and was taken up dead.

Another version says that when they picked him up, he was dead. Here it is after all that preaching, and after Eutychus falling, they look at Eutychus and they pronounce him dead. Notice they do not try to do anything to change his condition. There is no CPR. There are no rescue efforts. They look at Eutychus after falling out of the window, and his unconsciousness is determined to be his death. Now, I am not trying to suggest that Eutychus was not dead. Perhaps, he was. But the point is that there was no effort by those around him to bring him back to life. He was determined dead and that was it! And spiritually that happens to many of us. Let us fall, especially when it comes to sin, we are pronounced dead and there is no opportunity for repentance. Think about how many scandals have rocked on Jesus Christ today because somebody fell. Think of all the popular televangelists who are no longer celebrated because of their fall. Think of people we know who have been discounted and disregarded because of their mistakes or their outright sins. We have killed people before their time. Even some of us have been looked at differently because of some of the things we have said and some of the things we have done. Some of us have been dis-counted because we didn't measure up to somebody's standard. But thank God that it's not over until God says it's over. Pastor Keith Marshall, Macedonia, Trenton preached this text at the Community Revival (4/27/14); he said every fall isn't forced. Every fall isn't fatal and every fall isn't final. In other words, there are some things I choose to do that can cause me to fall short of God's glory. But in my fall, it doesn't mean that I'm died. Neither does that mean that I can't get up again!

(CLOSE) And that's all I'm trying to say today, Regardless of how far you've fallen in life. For Eutychus, it may have been 3 stories, but for you, your fall may have been over 3 days. Your fall may have over 3 months; your fall may have been 3 years. The encouragement of the text is that there is still life in you. The Bible says,

> *10 And Paul went down, and fell on him, and embracing him said, Trouble not yourselves; for his life is in him.*

And that's really where I want to close this message. They drew the wrong conclusion. You see, they just picked him up, but Paul embraced him. Paul laid hold of him. And Paul had the faith to believe that God was able to raise this young man back to life.

And unlike the other accounts of the resurrection, it is not clear how his life came back to him. All we know is that he was taken up dead by one group, but when Paul came down and assessed the situation, Paul said, "There is still life in him."

And that's where I want to close. Don't let anybody make the wrong assumption about your life. Don't let anybody kill you before your time. Don't let anybody write you off when God is still calling your name.

There is still life in you!

Thank God He Fell Asleep In Church   Dr. Willie J. Thompson Jr.

Acts 20:7-12 (NRSV)

7 On the first day of the week, when we met to break bread, Paul was holding a discussion with them; since he intended to leave the next day, he continued speaking until midnight. ⁸There were many lamps in the room upstairs where we were meeting. ⁹A young man named Eutychus, who was sitting in the window, began to sink into a deep sleep while Paul talked even longer. Overcome by sleep, he fell to the ground three floors below and was picked up dead. ¹⁰But Paul went down, and bending over him took him in his arms, and said, 'Do not be alarmed, for his life is in him.' ¹¹Then Paul went upstairs, and after he had broken bread and eaten, he continued to converse with them until dawn; then he left. ¹²Meanwhile they had taken the boy away alive and were not a little comforted.

Thank God He Fell Asleep In Church

While Matthew, Mark, Luke and John provide for our engagement the four different versions of the Life and ministry of Jesus Christ; only the one book of Acts gives us an account of the life of the early church. The Book of Acts is unique because it is our primary window into the world of the first Christians, the very first believers to live in the age of grace under the power of the indwelling Holy Spirit. And while we are eager to see what the early church was really like, Acts reminds us that it was not a perfect church. What we learn from acts is

> *We serve a perfect God who is faithful to work through real people and real situations to accomplish his glorious purposes.*

that we serve a perfect God who is faithful to work through real people and real situations to accomplish his glorious purposes.

So many people look for the perfect church, but Acts is a reminder that there is no perfect church. There is no church lacking nothing, complete in its nature or kind. There is no church without defects or blemishes. There is no church completely suited for a particular purpose or situation. There is no one excellent and delightful in all respects. There is no church completely flawless, faultless and free of defects. And anywhere you find a church, meaning a called out group of people, a local congregation of Christian believers, rather in Jerusalem, Antioch, Ephesus, Corinth, Rome, Clairton, Asia or in Achaia you will find a group of imperfect people serving a perfect God, who chooses to use imperfections, to carry out His perfect purposes.

Look for it and you will see a fingerprint on the doorknob. Look for it and you will see a grain of sand in the carpet. Look for it and you will see a piece of paper in the trash can? Look for it and you will find a crack in the wall and a book out of place? If you look a little harder you will see that one ear is bigger than the other. If you look harder you will see that one eye doesn't open up all the way like the other? If you look and see one leg is shorter than the other? But the blessing is that God uses the imperfect to manifest his perfect purposes.

And Luke is writing with the intent to help us understand that the only way God does this is through His precious gift called the Holy Spirit. So Acts is not only about the acts of the apostles, it's about the Acts of God through the Spirit filled Apostles in His church. Acts is about how God continues to work out his redemptive purposes through the church.

Lets share this announcement: God has launched his extended buy-back program and the dealer is God's church. And even though imperfect, when empowered by the Holy Spirit, God's Church and God's people are the one with the message of hope, that offers the way for humanity to come back to God. Some people say I don't need to go to church. Some people say I don't need to be in church to believe in God. And Acts opens up and Paul declares, "yes but, have you received, since you believed?" Have you gotten the power needed to become witnesses to what you believe? And to be a witness is not when you just saw what happened, at that point you are a spectator, you become a witness, when you have the power to say I saw it for myself and now let me tell you what happened.

And God's church is the way and the avenue for you to be empowered with your imperfections to participate in the purposes and redemptive buy-back plan of God. And not just in your neighborhood, God's power comes to take you to the uttermost parts of the earth, with your imperfect self. Your job is not just to be saved, your assignment is to spread the Good news of Jesus Christ and His message, his buy back program to every part of the earth. And the only way you ever get up and get the confidence to go is through the indwelling of the HOLY GHOST. And that's when Revival breaks out. Not just when you come to church, but When you carry the church wherever you go and Be My Witnesses, so saith the Spirit of God.

Again every group of called out believers, have imperfections but God uses those imperfections to accomplish his redemptive purposes. For instance, take our text, being the skilled physician that he is, Luke gives us great details surrounding the 24 hour expository preaching and teaching moment of Paul the night before he leaves Troas, a city of Mysia, Asia Minor, on the seacoast, about ten miles south of the entrance city founded by Alexander the Great. Paul is having church around the clock, empowered by the Holy Spirit to share the Word of God with people, whom he may not see again. A young man named, "Eutychus (meaning "fortunate"), who was seated in the window, drifts asleep and falls from the third story window to his death. Paul rushes down stairs, and God uses (that long winded Holy Ghost filled preacher) to raise this young man from the dead. The group continues back up stairs where they share a meal (probably including the Lord's supper) and listen to Paul until daylight, when it is time for him to leave.

> *Every group of called out believers, have imperfections but God uses those imperfections to accomplish his redemptive purposes.*

And as we see the story, we note things which we would consider imperfections (can you hear the folk talking); first the Long winded, Holy Ghost Preacher. Second, the flickering light of the candle. Third, the overcrowded room, or parking lot, which caused people to have to sit in the window. Fourth, the food is getting cold, because we are waiting for them to stop having church. Fifth, He is still preaching, Sixth, people are going to sleep. Seventh, we need some more light in here. Eighth, people falling asleep. Ninth, the green beans are getting cold. Tenth, people are falling asleep. Eleventh, That boy fell out the window.

233

Twelfth, He died yall. Next, he interrupted the service. Now the pastor got to go out there and deal with this. Next, Our insurance don't cover this. Next, the chicken is getting cold. Next, he is a preacher, he ain't no doctor. Yall just gonna take his word and go back to church? Yall a insensitive church. Now yall wanna eat. Is he preaching again? So is he alright? Well let him preach, he is leaving tomorrow anyway!.

See all the imperfections that may arise just in between verse 7 and verse 12. But I Thank God He Fell Asleep In Church. And if we can draw from it literally, let us look at its metaphorical contribution.

I thank God he fell asleep in church, because when he fell, somebody there went down to where he was.

The Bible says Paul stopped his message, and went down to see about the young man. And the blessing of being a part of God's church, is that when you are down even if you fall, somebody ought to come and see about you. In God's church, instead of condemning people when they are down and instead of judging people when they fall, God's church shows up to see about you in your time of need. We can't just let people fall or be away or get sick or hit hard times and feel discouraged and not go and see about them. And we can just sit back and wait for people to come to us, like we are their salvation. Jesus calls us to go and see about people and find them. I thank God he fell asleep in church, because somebody didn't just stay away and turn up their nose, they went down to where he was. And sometimes the church is going to have to start showing up in some Down places. We have to leave the comfort of our cushioned pews, and leave the enchantment and charm of our church titles and the fellowship only found in our four walls and go to some down places. It's time to turn our noses down and go down and see about the people who have fallen down around town. I thank God he fell asleep in church, because at least somebody was there and went down to where he was.

Not only that but if we give credence to its metaphorical value, Paul stopped preaching, went down to where he was, bent over him and took him in his arms. So I thank God he fell asleep in church, because when he fell, somebody there embraced him in their arms.

Do you know the power of a simple hug? Research proves that hugs generate the hormone called oxytocin, known as the "Get Along Hormone." Hugging produces the things needed to help us learn how to bond. Further research proves that hugs are non verbal communication, that expresses love, sympathy, friendship, familiarity and affections. In fact studies show that folks who hug regularly have reduced heart rates, lower blood pressure, increased nerve activity and better moods. A survey of successful marriages, even showed that hugging and touching (not intimate this time) were key factors in keeping the relationship long lasting. Hugging helps build better bonds with people, reconnects the mind to the body, cultivates patience and makes you a better hugger. I'm glad he fell asleep in church, because when he fell somebody there went down and threw their arms around him even though he was picked up dead. You ought to every now and then hug somebody. Everybody needs a hug, it may save their life, it communicates love, sympathy, friendship, familiarity and affection.

And according to research conducted by Patricia McConnel the only primate that does not enjoy being hugged is a dog. Because canines interpret putting a limb over another animal as a sign of dominance. But we are all people,

> *Don't just come see about me, throw your arms around me and hug me.*

up in here and we all need somebody, when we fall to embrace us. Don't just come see about me, throw your arms around me and hug me. If I stink, hug me, If I'm dirty, hug me. If you mess up your clothes and your reputation, when I'm down, throw your arms around me and show me some love. Change my mood, Lower my heart rate and chill me out not with words, but with a simple hug. I'm glad he fell asleep in church, because when he felt somebody embraced him even though he was picked up dead.

And lastly, if we can draw something from the metaphorical contribution of this great story found in the book of Acts. A record of a brother who fell asleep in church, interrupted the service made the preacher come down to where he was and the preacher threw his arms around him and the tenth verse tells us, Paul said, "Do not worry, he's alive." I'm glad he fell asleep in church because when he fell, there was somebody there who knew he was alive, even though he fell dead.

And that's why you need God's church, because in God's church, there will always be somebody who can speak life into a dead situation. Paul says, Don't worry, He's alive. But we just saw him fall three stories to the ground dead. We just had some of the crew pick him up and he was dead. We did not see him breathing, and he was not moving, Paul, he was dead. But Paul says Don't worry, he's alive.

And sometimes you will get into some situations where it looks like you will never make it out of. And sometimes you will grab ahold of some things that will literally rob you and leave you for dead. Sometimes you will go through some hardships and trials that will take the very life out of you. But if you can make it to God's church, somebody there ought to be able to speak life into a dead situation. Paul said, "Don't Worry, He's Alive!" You have got to get yourself to a church that speaks life and not death. You have to get yourself to a church that has the power of God in them to talk you back into existence. And I'm not talking about brick and mortar. I'm talking about somebody, who is not focused on their imperfections, but who will allow a perfect God to use their imperfections, for God's redemptive purposes. I'm glad he fell asleep in church, because somebody there spoke life in the midst of death. Somebody there spoke health in the midst of sickness. Somebody there spoke wealth in the midst of poverty. Somebody there spoke testimony in the midst of the test. Somebody there spoke peace in the midst of confusion. Somebody there spoke revival in the midst of dry bones. Somebody there spoke unity in the midst of division.

> *I'd rather fall asleep in Gods' church than in those mean streets.*

Why? Because It Works. God's church is the answer. How do I know, because The Bible says that after speaking, they all went back up stairs and ate the Lord's Supper together. And Paul kept on Preaching until dawn and then he left. And meanwhile, the young man was taken home unhurt and everyone was greatly relieved. When you fall asleep in God's Church, somebody there will come down to where you are, somebody there will embrace you and somebody there will speak life into you even though you fell dead. I'd rather fall asleep in Gods' church than in those mean streets.

Some people say it's rude to fall asleep in church. It's rude to sleep while the sermon is going on. But you gotta be careful when defining sleep. Because there are some people who are asleep with their eyes wide open. There are some people who sleep with a song on their lips and a dance on their feet. They are wide awake but they are SLEEP to what God is doing right in front of them. Snoozing on God. Taking a power nap in the midst of the battle. That when you do suspend activity real quick with the intent to jump right back in once you have been refreshed. Sleep on God. Some folk are getting their beauty rest. Too pretty to help somebody. Too dainty to pick up some trash and shake a hand. Sleep right here in the church. But the Blessing of Falling asleep in church is that at least you will have somebody nearby and in a quick moment, nudge you, and say wake up, if you fall asleep. At Least you have somebody near to say Wake Up. And that is what I need, somebody to nudge me when they see me dozing off. I need somebody to nudge me when they see I'm headed in the wrong direction., I need somebody to "nudge me," when they see I'm snoozing and should be up and ready for the battle. I might get a little attitude when you do it… but pay me no mind and nudge me. Bump me, say something to me. Don't let me fall to my death. But nudge me and tell me to wake up. Thank God He fell asleep in church.

And not just in the here and now but also in the life everlasting. I know that if I fall asleep down here, I will wake up over there, where Job declares the wicked will cease from troubling. And the weary soul would be at rest. For in my Father's house are many mansions, Jesus said if it were not so I would not have told you.

Notice, while in the church the young man fell dead, but he didn't stay dead. Doesn't that remind you of another young man? Except this young man wasn't at the church, he was the church. This 33 year old young man, on a hill called Calvary, nailed to an old rugged cross, and the Bible says, He fell dead, But he didn't stay dead. Early Sunday Morning, He got up with all power in his hand. And his Get Up, relieved everybody from sin, hell, death and the grave. You see the church is in revival when Everybody, gets relief and not just a few folk.

It's Revival, Thank God, He Fell Asleep In Church.

-REFERENCES-

King James Version (KJV)

The Message Bible (MSG)

New Living Translation (NLT)

New Revised Standard Version (NRSV)

Contemporary English Version (CEV)

www.reddit.com

-ABOUT THE AUTHORS-

Reverend John H. Gamble Jr. is a passionate pastor, preacher, bible teacher, and worship leader whose multifaceted gifts have afforded him numerous opportunities to minister across denominations, both nationally and abroad. Since 2003, he has served as the Pastor of Smyrna Missionary Baptist Church in Newark, New Jersey. In addition, he has held several leadership positions in both the North Jersey District Missionary Baptist Association (currently Moderator) and General Baptist Convention of New Jersey, Inc.

A public school educator for over two decades, Rev. Gamble has taught both elementary and middle school, and has held instructional leadership positions including, Principal, Vice Principal, and Director of Curriculum and Instruction. He is a graduate of Rutgers University with a Bachelor of Arts degree in History and Africana Studies, St. Peter's College with a Master of Arts degree in Educational Leadership, and twice from Drew University Theological School with Master of Divinity and Master of Sacred Theology degrees.

A lifelong New Jerseyan, Rev. Gamble is a proud member of Alpha Phi Alpha Fraternity, Inc. and is actively engaged in advocacy for marginalized communities through his professional and religious affiliations through his work with civic, non-profit and grassroots organizations.

Willie J. Thompson Jr. Ph.D., serves as Senior Pastor and Teacher of Oak Grove Baptist Church. Prior to becoming senior pastor and teacher, Pastor Thompson had the privilege of serving the Oak Grove community for over 20 years. He also served as youth and young adult pastor at

Prince George's Community Presbyterian Church, Senior Pastor & Teacher of the Morning Star Baptist Church, and President and Founder of both In His Presence Ministries, Inc. and W. J. Thompson, Jr. Ministries, Inc. Dr. Thompson, is currently an assistant professor in the Sociology and Social Sciences department at Allen University and Dickerson Green Theological Seminary in Columbia, SC. His research interests include: sociology, religion, research methods, homiletics, leadership, religious experience, social psychology, inequality (race, gender & class) and urban development.

Thompson received his Baccalaureate Degree in Religion & Philosophy from Benedict College and Master's of Divinity and Doctor of Philosophy (Inequality & Urban Development) from Howard University in Washington, D.C. He has served the academic community for over a decade in several capacities, which include: Diversity Coordinator for the graduate division of the University of California San Diego, Assistant Professor of Sociology at Northern Virginia Community College, Lecturer at the University of Maryland, College Park; Keynote Speaker & Workshop Presenter at several national and international research conferences; Graduate & Divinity School Recruiter, Hearing Officer; Administration & Logistics Coordinator for the Howard University's Graduate Schools Office of Student Affairs & Activities and Office of Retention, Mentoring and Support. Dr. Thompson is a member of Kappa Alpha Psi Fraternity Inc., Alpha Kappa Delta Sociological Society, the Edward A. Bouchet Honor Society, the American Sociological Association and the American Academy of Religion. In the spring of 2020, Dr. Thompson was inducted into the Martin Luther King Jr., International College of Ministers and Laity at Morehouse College (Board of Preachers) in Atlanta, GA. Between 2002 and 2011 he helped to establish 8 congregations in Ghana, East Africa.

Willie is an author, couples coach, life coach and currently serves as the Chief Engagement & Strategy Officer of two multimillion-dollar service companies. He is an ordained minister and is the founder of two non-profit religious organizations committed to empowerment, education and outreach. Lastly, Dr. Thompson is President of Compass Consulting LLC., a minority owned enterprise that manages client engagement and strategy for businesses leading initiatives of social responsibility and multi-cultural communications.

Ingram Content Group UK Ltd.
Milton Keynes UK
UKHW021838140623
423408UK00014B/114/J